EVERY PERSON'S
GUIDE
TO THE
HIGH HOLY DAYS

EVERY PERSON'S
GUIDE
TO THE
HIGH HOLY DAYS

RONALD H. ISAACS

JASON ARONSON INC.
Northvale, New Jersey
Jerusalem

26490

This book was set in 12 pt Weiss by Hightech Data Inc., of Bangalore, India and printed and bound by Book-mart Press, Inc. of North Bergen, NJ.

"Pope Elhanan," "Rabbi Amnon of Magence," "Two Socks on One Foot," "A Mother's Prayerbook," "A Crying Baby," and "Begin with Yourself," are reprinted from *The Classic Tales: 4,000 Years of Jewish Love* © 1989 by Ellen Frankel (Jason Aronson Inc.).

Library of Congress Cataloging-in-Publication Data

Isaacs, Ronald H.
    Every person's guide to the High Holy Days / Ron Isaacs.
      p. cm.
    Includes bibliographical references and index.
    ISBN 0-7657-6018-5
    1. High Holidays. 2. Mahzor. High Holidays. 3. High Holidays—Liturgy. 4. Judaism—Liturgy. I. Title.
BM693.H5173 1998
296.4'31—dc21   98–38761

Printed in the United States of America. Jason Aronson Inc. offers books and cassettes. For information and catalog write to Jason Aronson Inc., 230 Livingston Street, Northvale, NJ 07647-1726, or visit our website: http://www.aronson.com

For Leora

CONTENTS

Contents

Contents

Contents

INTRODUCTION

Rosh Hashanah, the Jewish New Year, and Yom Kippur, the Day of Atonement, are known in Jewish tradition as the *Yamim Noraim*—the Days of Awe. Rosh Hashanah is the beginning and Yom Kippur is the culmination of the ten special awe-inspiring days within which Jews are afforded the opportunity of a spiritual recovery by strenuous personal effort. Whereas most Jewish holidays celebrate national events in Jewish history, on these holy days Jews are instructed to scrupulously examine their deeds and more significantly their misdeeds during the preceding year. Rosh Hashanah and Yom Kippur's goal is nothing less than an ethical and religious reassessment of one's life. On the Days of Awe, Jewish tradition teaches, God decides who shall live and who shall die during the coming year. The liturgical prayers attempt to influence God's decision.

On the so-called High Holy Days, the synagogues are filled to capacity, and in many congregations there are overflow services to accommodate the vast numbers for whom no seats would otherwise be available. The multitudes of worshippers hold in their hands a book called the *Machzor* containing the liturgy of Rosh Hashanah and Yom Kippur.

For Jews lacking the knowledge of the High Holy Day liturgy, the *Machzor* remains a "sealed book" whose grandeur and sublimity are by and large uncomprehended. It would be in accord with sound pedagogic practice to make this book a vehicle for a more profound understanding of the basic teachings of Judaism.

This volume is intended to help people prepare and participate in the High Holy Days. The goal is to be basic but comprehensive, providing both home and synagogue observances that are essential to the Days of Awe. The volume will also include the many customs related to High Holy Day preparation during the month of Elul preceding the Days of Awe; a chapter on the shofar and its significance; reference to the *Selichot* penitential prayers and the meaning of sin, confession, and repentance in Jewish tradition; explanations of the basic prayers found in the *Machzor* and a variety of topics related to both Rosh Hashanah and Yom Kippur (including the background of each holiday, home celebrations, laws and customs, the holidays as they appear in the Talmud and Midrash, short stories related to these holidays, and Rosh Hashanah and Yom Kippur quotations). These is also a Days of Awe glossary and a section that includes books for further study.

I hope that you will find this book a useful guide in your preparation and celebration of the High Holy Days. Perhaps it will assist you in observing them in your home and in the synagogue with greater devotion and much joy.

—Rabbi Ronald Isaacs

ONE

PREPARING FOR THE DAYS OF AWE

Rosh Hashanah does not simply burst in upon us. Because of the great solemnity surrounding the High Holy Days, a whole month, called Elul, was ordained as a preparatory period. The period concluded on Yom Kippur, and later in history extended to *Hoshanna Rabbah*, the seventh day of the festival of Sukkot. A hint regarding the length of this period is found in the forty days that Moses, according to the Bible's account, spent in heaven before receiving the second set of tablets. These forty days started on the first of Elul and ended on Yom Kippur. (*Pirke de Rabbi Eliezer*, 46)

This chapter will enumerate some of the customs and observances that have been adopted for the month of Elul to accentuate the theme of repentance and help one better prepare his or her mind and heart for the Days of Awe.

THE MONTH OF ELUL

Following are the array of customs and traditions related to the period of preparation for the Days of Awe during the month of Elul:

1. The mystic Rabbi Isaac Luria said: "it is written [Exodus 21:13]: 'And if a man lie not in wait, but God cause it to come to hand, then I will appoint you.' The initials of the last Hebrew four words, אנה לידן ושמתי לך, spell out Elul אלול, to signify that this is a propitious month to repent for the sins that one has committed the entire year. It further indicates that during this month, one should also repent for sins committed unwittingly."

Others, who interpret the Torah metaphorically, said of the verse [Deuteronomy 30:6]: "And God will circumcise your heart and the heart of your seed," that the initials of the four words: את לבבך את לבבך spell out Elul (אלול). Also, the initials of the verse [Song of Songs 6:3]: "I am my beloved's and my beloved is mine," אני לדודי דודי לי) spell out Elul (אלול). Likewise the initials of the verse [Esther 9:22]: "One to another and gifts to the poor (איש לרעהן ומתנות לאביונם) spell out Elul (אלול). This is a reference to the three things, namely repentance, prayer, and charity, which should be diligently practiced during this month. "God will circumcise" implies repentance; "I am my beloved's" refers to prayer, for prayer is a song; "One to another and gifts to the poor" indicates charity.

2. It is the custom to sound the shofar daily (except on the Sabbath) during the month of Elul, beginning the second of *Rosh Chodesh* and continuing daily after the morning service. The *tekiah*, *shevarim*, and *teruah* sounds are blown on the shofar. The reason for sounding the shofar during the month of Elul is to move people to repentance, for the sound of the shofar has the quality to stir the hearts of people.

3. It is the practice to recite Psalm 27 at the conclusion of both morning and evening services during the month of Elul, beginning

with the first day of Elul and concluding on *Hoshanah Rabbah.* Psalm 27 is a plea to God for help when we are bested by enemies around us. The practice of reading it at this time is based on a midrash (Psalm 27:4), which interprets the first verse of the psalm as follows: "The Lord is my light" on Rosh Hashanah, "my salvation" on Yom Kippur, and "whom shall I fear" on *Hoshanah Rabbah.*

4. When writing a letter to a friend, the custom is to add a note of prayer at the beginning or the end of the letter on behalf of one's friend's well-being for the coming year.

5. It is customary to examine tefillin (phylacteries) and mezuzot during the month of Elul, in order to rectify any defect or error found in them.

6. In generations of old it was customary for the shamash (synagogue attendant) to proclaim daily during the month of Elul in the synagogue: "Return, you wayward sons."

SELICHOT (PENITENTIAL PRAYERS)

Selichot, or penitential prayers, are recited before the morning service during the month of Elul and between Rosh Hashanah and Yom Kippur. Sephardic Jews begin reciting these penitential prayers on the first day of Elul; Jews of Ashkenazic origin usually begin reciting them on the Sunday before Rosh Hashanah.

According to the Code of Jewish Law, there should be at least four days during which the Selichot prayers are recited. One of the reasons for this is that a sacrificial offering in the Temple was examined for four days for defects or blemishes that would disqualify it from being sacrificed. A person should consider himself to be like a sacrificial offering on Rosh Hashanah and hence needs four days for self-examination.

In America, it has become traditional custom to hold the first *Selichot* service on Saturday night after midnight. Since people are in the habit of staying up late on Saturday nights, it is easier for them to attend such services than to rise early the next morning. Another commendable custom is to have a study session during the hours preceding *Selichot* at which some aspect of the meaning and purpose of the High Holy Days is discussed.

The Selichot service is a collection of penitential prayers, the work of liturgical poets called *paytaneem* who flourished during the ten centuries following the close of the talmudic era. The structure of the service follows a definite pattern. Originally the service consisted of several groups of biblical verses, each climaxed by the recitation of the thirteen attributes of God found in Exodus 34: 6–7. Through the centuries the service has been expanded, and today the standard form is to start with Psalm 145 and end with the prayer *Shomer Yisrael* (Guardian of Israel). A collection of biblical quotations, the thirteen attributes and their introductory prayers, the short confession *ashamnu*, and some concluding prayers are the constant of each service. The variables are the *piyyutim* (liturgical poems), as different ones are recited each day.

EREV ROSH HASHANAH—THE DAY BEFORE ROSH HASHANAH

On the Sabbath preceding Rosh Hashanah the prayer for the new month, which would normally be recited, is omitted. The purpose of this prayer is to announce when the new month begins, and according to the Code of Jewish Law it is not necessary to do so when the beginning of the new month is also Rosh Hashanah. Folklore has added another reason for the omission, that of confusing Satan. In rabbinic thought, Satan is waiting for Rosh Hashanah in order to speak ill of the children of Israel before the throne of judgment. The omission of the prayer for the new month will therefore work to mislead Satan about the date, and thus Satan will miss his chance!

The day before Rosh Hashanah has a special cluster of customs and observances all its own. Following is a brief of summary of the more noteworthy ones:

1. The *Selichot* penitential prayers are more extensive than on other mornings. Even a bereaved person who is sitting shiva and thus would normally stay home may leave his house in order to join the congregation in the synagogue to say the *Selichot* penitential prayers.

2. In some congregations, there is a procedure called *hattarat nedarim*—releasing from vows, which takes place after services. The person who wants to be released from vows that he may have forgotten about should declare so in the presence of three who constitute a court. Then the court releases the person from these vows.

3. It is customary to replace the cover of the Torah reading table, the Torah covers, and the Ark curtain cover with white ones. White is the symbol of atonement and grace.

4. It is customary after morning services on the day before Rosh Hashanah to visit the graves of loved ones and pledge charity in their memory.

5. The practice of sending greeting cards to friends wishing a happy new year is also commendable. Originally it was customary to wish each one that he or she be inscribed in the Book of Life.

6. Bathing and getting one's hair cut is also a traditional way of honoring the festival.

7. It is customary in traditional circles to fast on the eve of Rosh Hashanah till after midday. Rabbinic tradition asserts that a third of one's sins are forgiven because of this fast.

TWO

THE SHOFAR

A BRIEF HISTORY

The shofar, the ram's horn, is the oldest surviving type of musical wind instrument, mentioned frequently in the Bible (sixty-nine times), in the Talmud, and in post-talmudic literature.

The shofar is first mentioned in Exodus 19:16 at the revelation at Mount Sinai. The Bible states that "on the third day, there was thunder, and lighting, and a dense cloud upon the mountain, and a very loud blast of the horn, and all the people who were in camp trembled." The shofar was also used to proclaim the Jubilee Year and the proclamation of "freedom throughout the land" (Leviticus 25:9–10), the verse that is engraved upon the Liberty Bell in Philadelphia, Pennsylvania. The shofar was also sounded on Rosh Hashanah (the Jewish New Year), which in the Bible (Numbers 29:1) is designated as *yom teruah* (a day of the blowing). It was also used as an accompaniment to other musical instruments (Psalm 98:6), in processions (Joshua 6:4ff), as a signal (II Samuel 15:10), as a call to war (Judges 3:27), and as a means to instill fear (Amos 3:6). Finally in the Bible, the shofar was sounded on the new moon, to usher in a new Jewish month. (Psalm 81:4)

In rabbinic literature we learn that it has been used to announce a death (Talmud, *Mo'ed Katan*, 27b), fast days (Talmud, *Ta'anit* 1:6), at excommunications (Talmud, *Mo'ed Katan* 16a), and at funerals. In the talmudic tractate of *Shabbat* 35b, we learn that the shofar was sounded six times on Friday afternoon at various intervals. At the first *tekiah* (single blast), the workers in the field ceased from their work. At the second, stores were closed and city workers ceased working. At the third, it was time to light the sabbath candles. The fourth, fifth, and sixth blasts (a *tekiah* [one blast], a *teruah* [nine short blasts], and again a *tekiah*) formally ushered in the holy sabbath.

In modern times, the shofar has been used at the various inaugurations of Israeli presidents. It was also used in 1967 to mark the liberation of the Western Wall in Israel after the Six Day War.

DESCRIPTION OF THE SHOFAR

Back in Temple times, when used in the ancient Jerusalem Temple, the shofar was sounded in conjunction with the *chaztozrah* (trumpet). In the Talmud (*Rosh Hashanah* 27a), we learn that the trumpet was made of silver while the processed horn was fashioned from the horn of one of five animals—sheep, goat, mountain goat, antelope, and gazelle—and used to fulfill the ritual obligation of the sounding of the shofar. The Talmud, however, prefers that the shofar be made of a ram's horn or wild goat's horn, because of its curved shape. According to the Talmud (*Rosh Hashanah* 3:2), a cow's horn may not be used because it is too much of a reminder of the episode of the golden calf, a negative historical event in the life of the Jewish people.

The shofar cannot be painted, though it is permissible for it to be gilded or carved with various artistic designs, as long as the mouthpiece is allowed to remain natural. If a shofar is found to have a hole in it, it is forbidden for use, although if none other is available it may be used. (Code of Jewish Law, *Orach Chayyim*, 586)

WHEN IS THE SHOFAR SOUNDED AND WHO MAY BLOW IT?

The shofar may be sounded during the daytime only. The person sounding the shofar is called the *ba'al tekiah* and anyone proficient and capable of blowing it may do so for the congregation. The prompter (i.e., the one who calls out the musical sounds to be blown) is called the *makri*. Women and children are theoretically exempted from the commandment to listen to the sounds of the shofar, but today most women and children are in attendance and do listen to it.

The shofar is not blown on the sabbath, the traditional reason being lest a person carry it from one domain to another, which is considered a violation of the sabbath according to talmudic law.

INSTRUMENTAL SOUNDS OF THE SHOFAR

During the month of Elul, the month that precedes the month of Tishri in which Rosh Hashanah, the New Year, falls, the shofar was blown as a kind of wake-up call from the second day of the new month to usher in the penitential season and prepare the Jew for the New Year.

On the New Year during services (the exception being when the New Year falls on the sabbath), the shofar is sounded. Originally the shofar could be sounded at any time during the course of the day on Rosh Hashanah. Sometimes it was sounded as early as dawn, in fulfillment of the rabbinic custom of hastening to perform a religious obligation. Rabbi Simeon ben Gamaliel II ordained that the sounding of the shofar ought to be postponed until the Musaf Additional Service. He made this decision because the Roman occupation troops in Palestine had once misconstrued the shofar blasts as a call to revolt, thereby killing many Jews. The delay until the Musaf Service enabled the Romans to observe how the Jews would pray for a considerable period of time before sounding the shofar, and this apparently convinced them that the sounding of the shofar was not meant as an act of war.

The first sounding of the shofar during the Rosh Hashanah service is generally preceded by the reading of Psalm 47. In some congregations, this psalm is read seven times, symbolic of the seven circuits that the Israelites made around Jericho before the wall fell down at the blasts of the shofar. This psalm is followed by seven more verses. Six of them form an acrostic, the first letters of which spell קרע שטן, meaning "destroy Satan," a mystical theme. Before the actual sounding of the shofar, the congregation's cantor recites two benedictions, the first praising God for commanding the Jews to listen to the sounds of the shofar, and the second, the *shehecheyanu*, praising God for the gift of life.

||| |≈| |≋|

תקיעה שברים תרועה תקיעה
תקיעה שברים תקיעה
תקיעה תרועה תקיעה

This diagram appears in the original manuscript of one of the oldest Hebrew prayer books in existence, that compiled by Saadia Gaon, the tenth-century Babylonian scholar. The diagram, read from right to left, is meant to represent the calls of the shofar. The

Hebrew words underneath the diagram are the names of the different calls in the order in which they are sounded during the synagogue service. Transliterated, the lines read:

Tekiah	Shevarim	Teruah	Tekiah
Tekiah	Shevarim		Tekiah
Tekiah	Teruah		Tekiah

The *tekiah* is one blast of the shofar that ends abruptly. The *shevarim* consist of three short sounds, and the teruah are a succession of tremulous sounds equal to three *shevarim.* On the festival of Rosh Hashanah, the sounds are arranged variously in the following combinations: *tekiah, shevarim, teruah; tekiah, shevarim, tekiah; tekiah, teruah, tekiah gedolah* (a prolonged *tekiah*).

A section of the Rosh Hashanah called the *Shofarot* verses is included in the additional Musaf Service, and consists of ten biblical verses in which the shofar is mentioned. The verses are as follows:

1. And it was on the third day, in the morning, there was thunder and lightning, and a dense cloud over the mountain; there was a loud shofar blast, and all the people in the camp trembled. (Exodus 19:16)

2. The sound of the shofar waxed louder and louder, and Moses spoke and God answered him. (Exodus 19:19)

3. And all the people perceived the thunders and the lightnings and the voice of the shofar, and the mountain smoking. And when the people saw it, they trembled and stood far away. (Exodus 20:15)

4. God manifested Himself with the sound of the shofar, God amidst the sound of the shofar. (Psalm 47:6)

5. With trumpets and sound of the shofar, raise joyful voices before God, the Sovereign One. (Psalm 98:6)

6. Sound the shofar on the new moon and on the full moon for our festive day. For it is a statute for Israel, a law of the God of Jacob. (Psalm 81:4–5)

7. Praise God, halleluyah. Praise God in the sanctuary, Praise God in the mighty firmament. Praise God for saving deeds, Praise God for God's greatness. Praise God with the blast of shofar. . . . (Psalm 150)

8. All of you inhabitants of the world and dwellers on earth. When a banner is lifted up on the mountain, see, and when the shofar is sounded, hear. (Isaiah 18:3)

9. On that day a great shofar shall be sounded. And they shall come who were lost in the land of Assyria. . . . (Zechariah 9:14)

10. On the day of your gladness, and on your festivals, and on new moons, you shall sound the shofar over your offerings. And they shall be to you a memorial before your God. I am God. (Numbers 10:10)

Toward the end of the Musaf Additional Service on Rosh Hashanah, some congregations follow the custom of again sounding the shofar to make a total of 100 blasts.

On the Day of Atonement at the end of the day the shofar is sounded one final time with a long shofar blast. All worshippers customarily together proclaim *"leshana ha'ba'ah be'yerushalayim"*— next year in Jerusalem.

REASONS FOR SOUNDING THE SHOFAR

There are a variety of reasons presented in rabbinic literature for the sounding of the shofar. According to the medieval philosopher Maimonides, the sounding of the shofar was the way of awakening the sleepers and a call to examine one's deeds and return in repentance. Yechezkel Kaufman, the biblical scholar, explains that the blowing of the shofar is man's means of expressing hope for salvation and awe and praise of God. Mordecai Kaplan, the founder of the Reconstructionist movement in America, explained that the sounding of the shofar was the summons of a person's soul to present itself before the judgment seat of God.

The most comprehensive explanation given for the sounding of the shofar was presented by the philosopher Saadia Gaon. He offered ten reasons for sounding it:

1. The sound of the "shofar" is analogous to the trumpet blasts that announce the coronation of a king. By sounding the shofar, we acknowledge God as King.

2. Rosh Hashanah is the first of the Ten Days of Penitence, and the shofar is sounded to arouse the consciences of people and induce them to return to God.

3. The shofar is a reminder of God's revelation at Mount Sinai, which was accompanied by the sounds of the shofar. It reminds us to pursue the study of Torah and practice our religious obligations.

4. The sound of the shofar is reminiscent of the exhortations of the prophets, whose voices rang out like a shofar in denouncing their people's wrongdoing and in calling them to the service of God and humankind.

5. The shofar is a reminder of the destruction of the Temple and calls upon us to strive for Israel's renewal of freedom.

6. The shofar is reminiscent of the ram offered as a sacrifice by Abraham to God in place of his son Isaac. It thus reminds us of the heroic faith of the ancestors of our people, who exemplified the highest devotion to God.

7. The shofar urges us to fall humble before God's majesty and might.

8. The shofar is our reminder of the Final Judgement Day, to call upon all people and all nations to prepare themselves for God's scrutiny of their deeds.

9. The shofar is a reminder of the call that will one day gather all of Israel's scattered people to return to the Holy Land.

10. The shofar is a reminder of the Day of Resurrection, the return to life, and the time when all people will proclaim that God is One and God's Name is One.

THREE

SELICHOT PENITENTIAL PRAYERS

The term *selichah* (plural *selichot*) literally means "forgiveness" and is thus applied to prayers for forgiveness. It is used to describe penitential prayers that are not generally an integral part of the service but are recited on certain solemn days of the Jewish calendar. Today, *selichot* is often used to refer to the prayers that are recited on the days preceding Rosh Hashanah, on the days between Rosh Hashanah and Yom Kippur, and on certain fast days.

ORIGIN OF *SELICHOT*

The synagogue service originally consisted mainly of biblical passages, selected and grouped to fit the occasion. The term selichot was at first applied to the verses selected for Yom Kippur, the Day of Atonement. Later, when to these verses were added other prayers of a penitential character, the whole was termed *selichot*.

The earliest of these other prayers in the selichot collections were very simple. One of them, beginning with the Hebrew words *mi she-anah* ("He shall answer us") is mentioned in the Talmud (*Taanit* 15) as having been recited in the service on fast days. Its theme is that just as God has answered His people on a variety of occasions throughout Jewish history, so too God will answer us in our prayers. Following is the prayer *Mi she-anah*:

He who answered our father Abraham in Mount Moriah, He shall answer us.

He who answered Isaac his son when he was bound on the altar, He shall answer us.

He who answered Jacob in Bethel, He shall answer us.

He who answered Joseph in prison, He shall answer us.

He who answered our forefather at the Red Sea, He shall answer us.

He who answered Moses at Horeb, He shall answer us.

He who answered Aaron with the censer, He shall answer us.

He who answered Pinchas when he rose from among the congregation, He shall answer us.

He who answered Joshua in Gilgal, He shall answer us.

He who answered Samuel in Mizpah, He shall answer us.

He who answered David and Solomon his son in Jerusalem, He shall answer us.

He who answered Elijah on Mount Carmel, He shall answer us.

He who answered Elisha in Jericho, He shall answer us.

He who answered Jonah in the belly of the fish, He shall answer us.

He who answered Hezekiah in his sickness, He shall answer us.

He who answered Hananiah, Mishael, and Azariah in the midst of the fiery furnace, He shall answer us.

He who answered Daniel in the lion's den, He shall answer us.

He who answered Mordecai and Esther in Shushan the capital, He shall answer us.

He who answered Ezra in captivity, He shall answer us.

He who answered all the righteous and pious, the perfect and the upright, He shall answer us.

Other well-known *selichot* are "We Have Sinned" (in Hebrew, *aval anachnu chatanu*) and the recital of the Thirteen Attributes of God.

According to the Mishnah tractate of *Taanit*, Chapter 2, the service on public fast days (such as the Tenth of Tevet or Fast of Esther) was opened with verses and prayers exhorting the worshippers to repentance. These may be regarded as the earliest *selichot* composed for use in the synagogue.

It is known that many *selichot* were composed before the seventh century of the common era. It is generally held that the lack of records of their composition is due to an early prohibition against copying holy writ, including prayers. At the request of the Spanish Jews of the ninth century, however, Rav Amram Gaon agreed to write down the daily prayers, together with some of the *selichot*, which were incorporated in his *siddur* (prayerbook).

At this period, apparently, *selichot* were said only during the Ten Days of Penitence and not, as is the present custom, also for a week before Rosh Hashanah. The extension of the use of *selichot* to the days before Rosh Hashanah was to provide a preparation for the Day of Judgment, and the ruling of Rav Hai Gaon shows that the Sephardim introduced such prayers for the entire month of Elul.

Many of the early *selichot* in present editions of *selichot* prayerbooks were composed in Italy. A number were composed in the communities of southern Italy under Byzantine rule in the ninth and tenth centuries. Especially noteworthy were the synagogal poets of the family of Amittai of Oria (whose compositions still feature prominently in the *Neila* service of the Day of Atonement).

The transmission of rabbinical learning, poetic skill, and mystical tradition, originally inspired by Babylonian Jewry, passed from southern Italy through central and northern Italy, the Rhineland and France, and is particularly associated with the family of Kalonymus. Among the liturgical poets of this family in the earlier period may be mentioned Rabbi Meshullam ben Kalonymus, who flourished at Lucca in the tenth century.

SUBJECT MATTER OF *SELICHOT* PRAYERS

Selichot prayers can be grouped, on the basis of subject, into four broad classes:

1. *Tochacha* (Admonition): Here the soul is called upon to consider its destiny and purpose. The themes are the shortness and vanity of life, the value of penitence, the Day of Judgment, the conflict between reason and passion, and the conflict between body and spirit.

2. *Akedah* (Sacrifice of Isaac): The poignant story of Abraham's attempt to sacrifice his beloved son Isaac forms the subject of many *selichot* prayers. In many cases the story is used to represent the martyrdom of the thousands of Jews who were sacrificed because they were the people of God. Each of them is likewise considered a sacrifice and their merit is invoked as a plea to God to forgive the sins of his people.

3. and 4. *Techinah* (supplication) and *Bakashah* (petition): These types of *selichot* represent the relationship between God and Israel. The wishes and desires of the individual are merged with those of the community as a whole, for it is not the individual alone who pleads but the congregation. Often in these plays the Angel of Mercy, the Torah, and the Throne of God are called upon to intervene on behalf of Israel.

SAMPLE *SELICHOT* PRAYERS FOR ROSH HASHANAH

Following are three sample excerpts of *selichot* prayers that are generally recited several days before the festival of Rosh Hashanah.

Supplication by Meir ben Isaac (1060)

Receive our prayer, and accept our supplication, instead of the sweet savor of the perpetual morning offering. Account it to those who rise to praise your name, as if they had succeeded in removing the ashes from the altar. Accept their worship in the sanctuary of their captivity ... Hearken to the reading and the order of our prayers, and the consumption of the limbs and fat pieces on the altar ... Cause our faces to shine toward the east, as the wood on the altar was placed eastward. May the arrangement of prayers with the recitation of the Thirteen Principles of Faith be pleasant to you, as the service of the pious priest when he twice arranged the pile of wood ....

Petition for Mercy by Rav Amram Gaon

Angels of mercy, usher in our petition for mercy before the God of mercy. Angels of prayer, cause our prayers to be heard before Him who hears prayer. Angels of supplication, cause our supplication to be heard before him who listens to supplication. Angles of tears, bring in our tears before the King, who is reconciled by tears. Multiply prayer and entreaty before the King, the most high God. Mention before him, and let him hear of the observance of the Torah and of the good deeds performed by those who repose in the dust. May he remember their love, and preserve their descendants, so that the remnant of Jacob perish not; for the flock of the faithful shepherd has become a disgrace. Israel the one people is a proverb and a byword. Hasten and answer us, O Lord our God, and redeem us from all harsh decrees, and save in Your abundant mercy your righteous anointed and Your people.

Petition for Kindness by Solomon ibn Gabirol

Our God and God of our fathers, I am appalled in my deep affliction at the day when my sins are visited; what shall I plead before my God? I am desolate and speechless when I remember how guilty I have been; I am even ashamed and confounded. My days are consumed in vanity; because of the shame of my youth, there is no peace within me. I am burnt with fever, now that the record of my debts is unfolded, and the creditor has come to exact payment. I cleaved in my darkness and my soul considered not that I am a stranger and a sojourner here. Woe to me when my day comes, then shall I awake from my dream, and return to my place. What excuse shall I render to him who sent me here, for my past sins and great transgressions? The pride of my heart has deceived me, and I was called from the womb for the iniquity which exhausted me. The fool imagines in his heart that he is like a tree planted by the brook, while he is to be carried to the grave. A vain delusion clings to him, which melts away when he turns here and there on his pilgrimage. He is cast about like a dumb stone, and carries nothing of all that he has into the grave. His strength did not support him at the time when his soul animated him, how much less when he is consumed with fire. My guilt ensnared me, indeed, my soul says so, during my existence on earth. Hence my soul is desolate, and like a person lying in disgrace, I must return home naked … When I am anxious for my sins, my thoughts reply to me, "Let us fall into the hand of God." Turn from the seat of your abode, and open your gates to me, for there is none beside you. O my Rock, defend me, and redeem me from my iniquity and teach me your law. Hear my voice according to your kindness, on the day when I shall stand before you, put not your servant away in anger. Look upon my affliction, and answer me. Behold, I am in your hand, and you, O God, be gracious to me. Send your truth and your kindness to the people who cry to you, and to me, even me, your servant. Forgive our guilt, and visit not the sins of our youth, for our days are but a shadow.

FOUR

THE MEANING OF SIN, CONFESSION, AND REPENTANCE IN JEWISH TRADITION

SIN IN BIBLICAL TRADITION

Various words are employed in the Bible to denote sin. Though they are often used interchangeably, their primary signification reveals the inner meaning of the biblical conception of sin. The word *chet*, used most frequently, connotes missing the mark. That is to say, the good action leads to a positive result, while the sinful action leads to no result. The term *avon* denotes something distorted and twisted, while the word *pesha* is derived from the verb "to rebel." In order that life should be kept intact, every sin brings its punishment, inflicted by the Author and Guardian of life.

The Book of Leviticus (4:1–35) describes the sin offering in great detail. Brought by one who had sinned, the sin offering differs from the others in the special treatment of the blood of the animal. The ritual takes two forms. If the sinner is the anointed priest, or if the offering expiates an offense of the entire community, the blood is taken into the holy place. Some of it is sprinkled toward the inner shrine, and some is placed on the horns of the incense altar. In such cases, the carcass of the animal is burned outside the camp. But, if the sinner is a secular ruler or a commoner, the blood is put on the horns of the main altar and the meat is eaten by the priests. In either case, the usual fat parts are burned on the altar.

Confession of sins was another means in the Bible of winning forgiveness. In this way the sinner expels the sin from his heart, showing at the same time that he does not intend to conceal his sin and to deceive God. The formula of the individual's confession of sins, expressed by the verb *chatati* ("I have sinned"), is found in the Bible some thirty times.

The formula of the national confession of sins in the Bible is expressed by the verb *chatanu* ("we have sinned"). This verbal form occurs some twenty-four times in the Bible.

Many times through scriptures the various words for sin connote errors in failing to fulfill one's obligation to God and God's covenant. The biblical doctrine of sin is thus described by the Prophet Jeremiah in Chapter 16:10-12 in the following way: "When you tell this people all this, and they say to you: 'Why has God threatened us with such terrible misfortune? What is our crime? What is the offense [in Hebrew, *chet*] we have committed against the Lord our God?'—then answer them: 'It is because your fathers forsook Me. They followed other gods, worshiping them and doing obeissances to them, and forsook Me and did not keep My law. And you have done even worse than they did, each following his own stubbornly wicked inclinations and refusing to listen to Me.'"

RABBINIC VIEWS OF SIN

The usual rabbinic term for sin is *averah*, from the root *avar* (to pass over; i.e., sin is a rejection of God's will). The rabbis rarely speak of sin in the abstract but usually of specific sins. There are sins of commission and omission—in the rabbinic terminology, the transgression of negative commandments and the failure to perform positive mitzvot. (Talmud, *Yoma* 8:8) Sins of commission are more serious than those of omission, (Talmud, *Yoma* 85:86a), and the term *averah* generally refers to the former. In one respect, however, the latter are more severe. If positive precepts have to be carried out at a certain time and that time has passed, the omission cannot be rectified. For example, the failure to recite the Shema on a particular day cannot be rectified.

Sins involving the transgression of negative precepts (the "thou shalt nots") are of two kinds—offenses against God and offenses against one's neighbor. The Day of Atonement brings forgiveness for sins committed against God (purely religious offenses). It only brings forgiveness for offenses against other human beings if the wrong done to the victim has first been put right. (Talmud, *Yoma* 8:9) The intention to sin is not reckoned as sin except in the case of idolatry. (Talmud, *Kiddushin* 39b)

Rabbinically speaking, sins are also divided into light and severe sins. The four most serious sins for the rabbis are murder, idolatry, adultery, and incest. It was eventually ruled that rather than commit these sins, a person must forfeit his life. (Talmud, *Sanhedrin* 74a) The light sins are those which "a person treads underfoot." (Tanchuma, Deuteronomy 8b)

Those who cause others to sin were severely castigated by the rabbis. One who causes another to sin is worse than one who slays him, because the murderer only excludes his victim from this life, while the one who causes another to sin excludes him from the life of the world to come. According to Ethics of the Fathers 5:18, Jeroboam is the prototype of the one who leads others to sin.

Sin is caused by the evil inclination (*yetzer ha'ra*), that evil force in humans that drives them to gratify their instincts and ambitions.

Strong expressions are used in rabbinic literature of the heinousness of sin and surrender to the evil inclination. For instance, Rabbi Simeon ben Lakish said: "Satan, the evil inclination and the angel of death are one and the same." (Talmud, *Baba Batra* 16a) It is said in the talmudic tractate of *Sukkot* 52b that the evil inclination entices man to sin in this world and bears witness against him in the world to come.

Rabbinic advice is given to people as to how they can rise above sin. For example, *Ethics of the Fathers* 2:1 says: One should know that above there is a seeing eye and a hearing ear and all of one's deeds are recorded in a book. The talmudic tractate of *Sotah* 1a states that the study of Torah and the practice of mitzvot are the best method of avoiding sin!

Following are some other rabbinic quotations related to sin and transgression:

1. Even a transgression is good in its season, if it is performed for the sake of God. (*Midrash, Ecclesiastes Rabbah* 3:2)

2. Whoever sins secretly thrusts away the Divine Presence. (Talmud, *Kiddushin* 31a)

3. To cause another person to sin is even worse than killing him. (*Midrash, Numbers Rabbah* 21)

4. Every sin of a person is engraved upon that person's bones. (Talmud, *Challah Rabbati* 3)

5. Akabiah ben Machalalel said: "I would rather be called a fool all of my life than sin for a single moment before God." (*Mishneh Eduyot* 5:6)

6. Rabbi Akiba said: "In the beginning a sin is like the thread of a spider's web. At the end, it becomes like a ship's cable." (*Midrash, Genesis Rabbah* 22:6)

7. To what may a sinner be compared? To one who beholds open handcuffs and places his hands into them. (Jerusalem Talmud, *Nedarim* 9:1)

8. It is better to sin out of good intentions than to conform with evil intent. (Talmud, *Nazir* 23b)

9. Three things sap a person's strength: worry, travel, and sin. (Talmud, *Gittin* 70a)

10. The biggest sin in the world is repeating anything without doing it in a new way. (Nachman of Bratslav)

CONFESSION

Jewish confession, addressed directly to God, is of no avail unless it expresses genuine feelings of regret and repentance. Rabbinic thinkers have compared the person who confesses his sin without repenting to a person who holds a defiled dead reptile in his hand while seeking ritual purification. (Talmud, *Taanit* 16a)

The most prominent confessions found in the prayerbook are the short and long forms of the confessionals in the High Holy Day *Machzor*. The catalogue of sins is listed alphabetically and in the plural, because the entire community is to regard itself responsible for the main offenses that could have been prevented.

Finally, traditional Jews also make confession on their deathbeds, in keeping with the rabbinic statement that "when a person is sick and near death, he is asked to make confession." (Talmud, *Shabbat* 32a)

Here are a variety of rabbinic statements and quotations related to the theme of confession:

1. One who confesses has a share in the world to come. (Mishneh, *Sanhedrin* 43)

2. If a person confesses his sins, he cannot be brought to judgment. (*Zohar* iv, 231a)

3. The person who confesses and forsakes his sins obtains mercy. (Talmud, *Taanit* 16a)

4. It is a good thing to confess to God. (Psalm 92:2)

5. Those who are put to death by the court have a share in the world to come, because they confess all of their sins. (Jerusalem Talmud, *Sanhedrin* 9:5)

6. Criminals are urged to confess within a short distance of the scene of execution. If they have nothing to confess, they are instructed to say: "Let my death be an atonement for all my sins." (Talmud, *Sanhedrin* 6:2)

REPENTANCE IN BIBLICAL TRADITION

The Hebrew word for repentance is *teshuvah*, which literally means to return to God. In Judaism, repentance is a prerequisite for divine forgiveness: God will not pardon people unconditionally but wait for them to repent. In doing repentance, a person must experience genuine remorse for the wrong that one committed and then convert his penitential energy into concrete acts.

The Bible is replete with idioms that describe man's active role in the process of repentance. The Book of Joshua 24:23 says "incline the heart to God," whereas the Book of Ezekiel 18:31 talks about making for oneself "a new heart." These two expressions of man's penitential activity are subsumed by one verb that dominates the Hebrew Bible—*shuv*—"return," which ultimately develops into the rabbinic concept of *teshuvah*, repentance. This root combines in itself both requisites of repentance: to turn from the evil and to turn to the good. The motion of turning implies that sin is not an unerasable stain but rather a wandering from the right path. Through the effort of "turning" to the right path, a power that God has given to all people, the one who transgresses can redirect his or her destiny.

The Haftarah, the prophetic portion that is read on the Sabbath between Rosh Hashanah and Yom Kippur, (called the Sabbath of Repentance) is taken in part from the Book of Hosea 14:2–10. Its opening words are "Return O Israel to God, for you have stumbled in your iniquity." Jeremiah the Prophet (3:1) warns "Return you backsliding Israel, says God." Ezekiel pleads, "Return you, and turn yourselves from all of your transgressions." When Jeremiah despairs of man's capability of self-renewal, he postulates that God will provide "a new heart" that will overcome sin and merit forgiveness. (Jeremiah 31:32–33) Throughout the Bible, even the worst sinner is always encouraged to believe that he can improve his ways, his sins being merely a temporary obstacle rather than a permanent mark on his character.

RABBINIC VIEWS OF REPENTANCE

The rabbis write and speak about repentance throughout rabbinic literature. Here is a cross-section of their comments that will help to provide insight into their thinking regarding the concept of repentance itself.

1. Repentance is one of the things created before the world itself. (Talmud, *Pesachim* 54a)

2. Repentance reaches to the very Throne of Glory, prolonging a man's life and bringing on the redemption. (Talmud, *Yoma* 86a, 86b)

3. God urges Israel to repent and not be ashamed to do so because

a son is not ashamed to return to the father who loves him. (*Midrash, Deuteronomy Rabbah* 2:24)

4. God says to Israel: "My sons, open for Me an aperture of repentance as narrow as the eye of a needle and I will open for you gates through which wagons and coaches can pass. (*Midrash, Song of Songs Rabbah* 5:2)

5. A twinge of conscience in a person's heart is better than all the floggings that such a person may receive. (Talmud, *Berachot* 7)

6. Rabbi Eliezer ben Hyrcanus said: "Repent one day before your death." His students asked him: "How is it possible for a person to repent one day before his death, since a person does not known when he will die?" He replied: "All the more reason is there that a person should repent every day, lest he die the next day. Thus, all his days will be days of repentance. (Talmud, *Avot de Rabbi Natan* 15)

7. Rabbi Simeon ben Lakish said: "Repentance induced by fear of consequences causes willful sins to be treated as unwitting. Repentance that springs from a nobler motive—love of God, causes willful sins to be treated as righteous deeds. (Talmud, *Yoma* 86b)

8. If a person repents and returns to sinning, that is no repentance. (*Pesikta Rabbati* 44)

9. Rabbi Meir said: "Great is repentance, because for the sake of one who truly repents, the whole world is pardoned. (Talmud, *Yoma* 86b)

10. In the place where penitents stand, even the whole righteous cannot stand. (Talmud, *Berachot* 34b)

11. One must not say to a person who has repented [and changed

his way of life], "Remember your former transgressions." (Talmud, *Baba Metzia* 58b)

12. Consider every day your last, and you will always be ready with good deeds and repentance. (Talmud, *Shabbat* 153a)

13. The gates of prayer are sometimes open, but the gates of repentance are forever opened. (*Midrash, Deuteronomy Rabbah* 2:7)

14. As long as the candle is still burning, it is still possible to make repairs. (Rabbi Israel Salanter)

15. How can one prove that one is truly penitent? Rabbi Judah said: "If an opportunity to commit the same sin presents itself on two occasions and one does not yield to it." (Talmud, *Yoma* 86b)

16. If a man stole a beam and built it into his house, he was freed from the obligation of demolishing the house and was allowed to pay for his theft in cash, in order to encourage him to repent. (Talmud, *Gittin* 5:5)

17. If robbers or usurers repent and wish to restore their ill-gotten gains, the spirit of the sages is displeased with the victims if they accept the restitution, for this may discourage potential penitents from relinquishing their evil way of life. (Talmud, *Baba Kamma* 94b)

18. If a person says: "I will sin and repent, and sin again and repent," that person will be given no chance to repent. (Talmud, *Yoma* 8:9)

REPENTANCE IN JEWISH PHILOSOPHY

Repentance was a popular topic in medieval ethical and philosophical writings. Saadia Gaon discusses repentance in the fifth section of his volume *Beliefs and Opinions*, while Bachya ibn Pakuda devotes the seventh "gate" of his volume *Duties of the Heart* to repentance. The great medieval philosopher Maimonides has an entire chapter in his *Mishneh Torah* that he devotes to the topic of the workings of repentance. These three philosophers agree that the essential ingredients of repentance are regret and remorse for the transgression committed, renunciation of the sin, confession and a request for forgiveness, and a promise not to repeat the offense. Maimonides, in particular, emphasizes the importance of verbal confession (*vidui*, in Hebrew), maintaining that one should publicly confess those sins that one has committed against one's fellow human being.

According to Bachya ibn Pakuda, the four conditions necessary for repentance are: 1. recognition of the evil nature of one's sin; 2. realization that punishment for one's sin is inevitable and that repentance is the only means of averting punishment; 3. reflections on the favors previously bestowed by God; and 4. renunciation of the evil act.

There are different gradations of repentance as well. According to Saadia, the highest level of repentance is the one that takes place immediately after one has sinned, while the details of one's sin are still before a person. A lower level of repentance is that which occurs when one is threatened by disaster. The very lowest is that which takes place before death.

According to Bachya, the highest level of repentance is the one where, while still capable of sinning, one has totally conquered his evil inclination. The next level is the repentance of one who, while managing to refrain from sin, is nevertheless constantly drawn toward sin by his evil inclination. The lowest form of repentance is the repentance of one who no longer has the power or opportunity to sin.

Maimonides writes in his *Mishneh Torah* of twenty-four things that hinder repentance:

Four of these are grievous offenses. If one commits any of them, God gives him no opportunity to repent because of the gravity of the offense. Offenders of this type are: 1. one who leads the people to sin; this includes one who prevents them from doing a good deed; 2. one who diverts another from the good to the evil, such as a seducer or enticer; 3. one who sees that his son is falling into bad ways and does not stop him; being under his control, the son would desist if checked by the father; hence, it is as if he actually led him to sin; 4. one who says: "I will sin and then repent." This includes one who says: "I will sin and Yom Kippur will atone."

Five of the twenty-four misdeeds shut the ways of repentance to those who commit them. They are: 1. one who stands aloof from the community; since he is not among them when they repent, he does not share the merit they attain; 2. one who opposes the rulings of the sages; since his opposition induces him to stay away from them, he remains ignorant of the ways of repentance; 3. one who makes a mockery of the divine precepts; since they are held in contempt by him, he does not eagerly obey them, and if he does not obey how can he attain merit? 4. one who insults his teachers; 5. one who hates rebukes, because he leaves himself no way of repentance; for it is reproof that induces repentance.

Five of the twenty-four misdeeds are of such nature that anyone who commits them cannot attain complete repentance, because they are sins against a fellow person without knowing who it is in order to compensate him and ask his pardon. Offenders of this category are: 1. one who curses the people and not an individual, of whom he might ask to forgive him; 2. one who shares with a thief; 3. one who finds lost property and does not announce it, that he may restore it to its owner; 4. one who despoils the poor, orphans, and widows; 5. one who takes bribes to tamper with justice, thus encouraging the bribing litigant and leading him to sin.

Five of the twenty-four offenses are such that the person who commits them is not likely to repent, because they are regarded by most people as trivial, with the result that the sinner imagines that it is no sin. Offenders of this class are: 1. one who shares a meal that is insufficient for its owner, since this is a tinge of robbery, one imagines that he has not done any wrong, saying: "I did not eat without his consent"; 2. one who makes use of a poor man's pledge, since a poor man's pledge happens to be only an ax or a plow, and the user says to himself: "The articles have not depreciated, and I have not robbed him"; 3. he who gazes at women lustfully supposes that there is nothing wrong in it, and does not realize that the lustful look is a grave sin, as it is written: "You shall not follow the desires of your heart and your eyes" [Numbers 15:39]; 4. one who elevates himself at the expense of another's degradation thinks to himself that this is no sin, since the other person is absent and has not endured shame; 5. one who suspects honest men says to himself that it is no sin. "What have I done to him?" he says; "is there anything more in it than a mere suspicion that maybe he has done it and maybe not?" He does not realize that it is sinful to regard a worthy person as a transgressor.

Five of the twenty-four misdeeds are such that anyone who commits them will always be attracted to them, and they are hard to be given up. One should therefore be careful lest he become addicted to them, for they are all extremely obnoxious traits. They are: gossip, slander, wrath, evil thought, and keeping bad company. In the rules concerning ethical behavior we have explained the traits that all people should ever cultivate, and so much the more one who repents.

All these and similar misdeeds do not prevent repentance, even though they hinder it. If a person is sincerely remorseful over them and repents, that person is indeed repentant and has a share in the world to come.

According to Maimonides, perfect repentance is where an opportunity presents itself to the offender for repeating the offense and that person refrains from committing it because of his repentance and not out of fear or physical inability.

Finally, according to Maimonides, repentance and Yom Kippur effect atonement only for sins committed against God, as when one has eaten forbidden food. Sins committed against one fellow human being, as when a person either injured or cursed or robbed his neighbor, that person is never pardoned unless he compensates his neighbor and makes an apology. Even though he has made the compensation, the wrongdoer must appease the injured person and ask his pardon. Even if only annoyed with him with words, one must apologize and beg his forgiveness. (Maimonides, *Mishneh Torah, Laws of Repentance,* Chapter 4)

According to Rabbi Yehuda He Chasid, a thirteenth-century ethicist, the following twenty-four obstacles block the road to repentance: 1. evil gossip; 2. talebearing; 3. anger; 4. thinking evil; 5. associating with the wicked; 6. partaking of a meal that does not even suffice for the host; 7. gazing at obscenity; 8. dividing stolen goods with a thief; 9. saying, "I will sin and then repent of this sin"; 10. saying, "I will sin, and Yom Kippur will procure atonement"; 11. disregarding one's teachers; 12. cursing the community; 13. discouraging your friend from doing a mitzvah and persuading him to sin; 14. making use of a poor person's pledge; 15. accepting a bribe to render a false judgment; 16. finding a lost object and not announcing it publicly so that it can be returned to its rightful owner; 17. seeing one's son fall into bad ways and not reprimanding him; 18. eating the loot taken from the poor and widows; 19. separating oneself from the community; 20. transgressing the words of the sages; 21. deriving honor from a friend's disgrace; 22. suspecting the innocent; 23. despising admonition; and 24. ridiculing the mitzvot. (*The Book of the Pious,* parag. 321)

REPENTANCE IN POSTMEDIEVAL PHILOSOPHY

The idea of repentance continued to play an important role in Jewish life in the postmedieval period. Those responsible for pogroms and expulsions often turned to Jews in turn to ask for forgiveness for sins that they assumed were at the root of their suffering. Messianic movements of this age also gave further incentive to a "returning" to God.

Lurianic mystics of this period associated repentance with the cosmic drama of redemption. For these kabbalists, repentance was an essential step in the process of *tikkun*—repair of the world. Through repentance, the Jews would be able to assist God in the elevation of the holy sparks entrapped in the shells, thus ushering in the age of messianic redemption.

The Musar ethical movement of the postmedieval period played up the factor of sin. For these ethicists, repentance became the daily task of each and every Jew. Especially during the month of Elul preceding the New Year, they spent their time in soul-searching. Some even went so far as to inflict suffering on themselves as self-punishment in an attempt to find perfect repentance.

REPENTANCE IN MODERN JEWISH PHILOSOPHY

In the modern period, which marked the assimilation of Jews and a drifting away from traditional forms of religion and belief in God, the idea of repentance appears in two attires. On the one hand, there is the traditional interpretation, which views repentance as something of which both the believing and nonbelieving Jew is in need. On the other hand, there is the reinterpretation of repentance as the way back to God for those who have weak roots in Judaism or have at some stage totally abandoned their roots.

The traditionalist interpretation takes its most original form in the philosophical writings of Abraham Kook, former Chief Rabbi of Israel, who devoted his work *Orot HaTeshuvah* to the subject of repentance. Kook weaves together three themes: the mystical idea that repentance is not only personal but partakes of cosmic proportions; messianic Zionism; and the "re-turning" of the individual to God. According to Kook's philosophy, when a person sins that person isolates himself from God, thereby disrupting the potential unity and harmony of all existence. Repentance is the overcoming of this isolation and communion with God, thus helping to re-establish harmony and peace in the universe.

Franz Rosenzweig, another twentieth-century philosopher, was on the verge of converting to Christianity when on the night of Yom Kippur in a small synagogue, he felt the fervor and spirit of the worshippers. It was on that night when he changed his mind and ultimately his entire life, returning to Judaism. For Rosenzweig, returning to God involves fulfilling the mitzvot, the religious obligations. Unlike Kook, who dealt with the subject of repentance in relation to Israel's return to God and nationhood, Rosenzweig was concerned with the turning away of the individual from Western culture, specifically Christianity, back to Judaism.

Finally, in the thought of the modern philosopher Martin Buber, a contemporary of Rosenzweig, the idea of repentance is the turning of the whole person to God.

FIVE

ROSH HASHANAH

*In the seventh month, in the first day of the month, shall be a
solemn rest to you, a memorial proclaimed with the blast of horns,
a holy convocation.*

—*Leviticus 23:24*

BACKGROUND

The *Zohar*, the most important book of Jewish mysticism, tells us
that Adam, the first human being, was created on Rosh Hashanah.
On that day Adam stood before God the Judge and repented for
all of his mistakes. God forgave him and then said to Adam: "So it
will be with your children. They will stand before me in judgement on Rosh Hashanah, and if they truly say they are sorry, I
shall forgive them." Rosh Hashanah provides us with our second
chance. It is a time for self-renewal and an opportunity to resolve
to become better people than those we were.

Marking the Jewish New Year with which Jewish chronology

begins, Rosh Hashanah occurs on the first day of the seventh month (Tishri), the holy month of the year just as the seventh day in the week is a holy day. Since early times Rosh Hashanah has been regarded as a day of reflection and repentance, essentially concerned with the individual and his ideal way on earth. Unlike the other historical-national festivals, beginning in the spring with Passover, and closing with Sukkot, the Festival of Booths in the fall, Rosh Hashanah (and Yom Kippur, too) are characterized by special solemnity and referred to as the *Yamim Nora'im* (Days of Awe), when all people stand before the divine throne for judgment.

Rosh Hashanah traditionally marks the creation of the world. Medieval writers noted that the letters of the word *bereshit* (בראשית), with which the Book of Genesis begins the account of creation, could be rearranged to read "aleph beTishri" א' בתשרי, the first day of the month of Tishri, when the Jewish New Year is celebrated.

ROSH HASHANAH IN
THE BIBLE

Rosh Hashanah is designated by four names, two biblical and two liturgical. In Leviticus 23:24, it is identified as a day of Sabbath observance (in Hebrew, *shabbaton*) and of shofar blasts as a reminder (in Hebrew, *zikaron teruah*). In Numbers 29:1 Rosh Hashanah is described as a day of sounding the shofar (in Hebrew, *yom teruah*). Liturgically, Rosh Hashanah is called *Yom ha-Din* (Day of Judgment) and *Yom ha-Zikkaron* (Day of Remembrance), when all people pass before the divine throne to give strict account of deeds committed during the year and to receive the promise of mercy by virtue of the ancestral kind deeds (known in Hebrew as *zechut avot*—merit of our ancestors) that are being remembered.

In the Bible, the name Rosh Hashanah is found only once, in

the Book of Ezekiel 40:1. In this passage it appears that Rosh Hashanah
is meant simply to refer to the beginning of the year, and not the
actual festival of Rosh Hashanah itself. The months of the year
were counted from the spring month Aviv (Exodus 12:2), later called
by the Babylonian name Nisan. The month known by the Babylonian
name Tishri is, therefore, called the "seventh month" in the Bible.
As previously noted, when the festival on the first of this month is
recorded, it is referred to as the festival of the seventh month, and
as a day of "memorial proclaimed with the blast of horns," or "a
day of blowing the horn." (Leviticus 23:23–25; Numbers 29:1–6) In
the Bible, the festival lasts for one day only; the two-day festival
arose out of the difficulty of determining when the new moon
actually appeared. Long ago, the beginning of a new month was
declared when two independent witnesses reported to the Sanhedrin
(rabbinical court) that the crescent of a new moon had appeared.
The declaration was relayed from city to city by lighting signal
fires on the hilltops. Sometimes false fires were lit by non-Jews who
wanted to confuse and delay the announcement of the new month.

To make certain that all the holidays were still celebrated on
their proper day even if this happened, an extra day was added to
Rosh Hashanah. As a result, Rosh Hashanah continues to be observed for two days by most Orthodox and Conservative Jews all
over the world, with the exception of Israel. The Reform and
Reconstructionist movements have generally chosen to defer to the
scientific exactitude of modern calendation, and thus observe one
day of Rosh Hashanah.

It has been conjectured that the Babylonian name of the month
Tishri is derived from the root seru, which means "to begin." The
ancient Semitic peoples thought of the year as beginning in the
autumn, at the time of the late harvest. This was the beginning of
the economic year, when crops began to be sold. It is plausible,

therefore, that the biblical Rosh Hashanah originally marked the beginning of the agricultural year. If this is correct, the rabbinic name Rosh Hashanah only makes explicit that which has been implicit in the observance of the day from earliest times. It was on the first day of the seventh month that Ezra the Scribe read the book of the Law before the people. (Nehemiah 8:1–8) The people, conscious of their shortcomings, were distressed to hear the words of the Law. But Nehemiah, Ezra's companion, said to them: "Go your way, eat rich viands, and drink the sweet beverages, and send portions to him who has none prepared. For this day is holy to our God. Do not be sad, for joy in God is your refuge." (Nehemiah 8:10)

The Psalmist is likely referring to the festival of Rosh Hashanah when he proclaims: "Blow the horn at the new moon, at the full moon for our festive day. For it is a law for Israel, an ordinance of the God of Jacob." (Psalm 81:4–5)

There have been other suggestions propounded as to the exact origins of Rosh Hashanah, including that of S. Mowinckel, who advanced the possibility of the existence of a pre-exilic autumnal New Year festival of the Israelites on which God was "enthroned" as King. He bases his claim on having found marked traces of this ancient festival in many of the psalms. Although others have accepted his theory, wide debate on the subject continues.

ROSH HASHANAH IN THE TALMUD

One of the Talmudic tractates in the order of *Moed* (Festivals) is that of Rosh Hashanah. Although the tractate does not deal exclusively with the festival of Rosh Hashanah, the opening *Mishneh* (*Rosh Hashanah* 1:1) speaks of four periods of the year, each known as Rosh Hashanah. The first of Nisan was designated as the New

Year for Jewish kings and for the religious calendar. The first of
the month of Elul was designated as the New Year for the tithing
of cattle. The first of Shevat was designated as the New Year for
trees. And the first of Tishri was designated as the New Year for
the civil calendar. It is a day when all people are judged.

Chapter 3 of the tractate *Rosh Hashanah* deals with particulars
of the ram's horn, known as the shofar in Hebrew. The chapter
includes a profound homily explaining that it is not the actual sound
of the ram's horn but its devotional effect, which is important. Chapter 4 first discusses whether the shofar is blown on the Sabbath
when Rosh Hashanah falls on that day. It then deals with the order
of benedictions for Rosh Hashanah, which are arranged in the Additional Musaf service.

In the Babylonian *Gemara* (*Rosh Hashanah* 10b–12a) there is a
discussion as to whether the world was created in the month of
Nisan or in Tishri. Rabbi Eliezer taught that the world was created
in Tishri, while Rabbi Joshua taught that it was created in Nisan.
Rabbi Eliezer's view seems to have been accepted in later amoraic
times, as reflected in the Rosh Hashanah prayers of those days.

Following is a cross-section of rabbinic comments related to the
festival of Rosh Hashanah:

1. Rabbi Nachman ben Isaac interprets the verse "from the beginning of the year even to the end of the year [Deuteronomy 11:12]
to mean that God determines at the beginning of the year what is
to be at the end of the year." (Talmud, *Rosh Hashanah* 8a)

2. On Rosh Hashanah heaven assigns to a person how much he
will earn during the coming year. (Talmud, *Betzah* 16a).

3. Confidence in God's mercy is expressed when it is said: "It is the
custom of men who appear before a court of justice to wear black

clothes, to let their beards grow long because the outcome is uncertain. But Israel does not do so. On the day of judgment, Rosh Hashanah, they wear white garments and have their beards shaven and they eat, drink and rejoice in the conviction that God will perform miracles for them." (Jerusalem Talmud, *Rosh Hashanah* 1:3, 57b)

4. The theme of God as King is particularly emphasized on Rosh Hashanah because of the day's association with God's judgment. (Talmud, *Berachot* 12b)

5. During the prayers on Rosh Hashanah, it is necessary to recite ten biblical texts that have the theme of God as King (in Hebrew, *malchuyot*, kingship verses); ten that have the theme of God who remembers (in Hebrew, *zichronot*, remembrance verses); and ten that have reference to the shofar (in Hebrew, *shofarot*, trumpet verses). (*Rosh Hashanah* 4:5–6)

6. Four names of the festival of Rosh Hashanah in rabbinic tradition are Rosh Hashanah, *Yom Teru'ah* (Day of Blowing the Horn), *Yom Ha-din* (Judgment Day), and *Yom ha-Zikkaron* (Day of Remembrance).

7. Rabbi Keruspedai said in the name of Rabbi Jochanan: Three books are opened on Rosh Hashanah, one for the completely righteous, one for the completely wicked, and one for the average person. The completely wicked are immediately inscribed in the book of death. The average persons are kept in suspension from Rosh Hashanah to the Day of Atonement. If they deserve well, they are inscribed in the book of life; if they do not deserve well, they are inscribed in the book of death. (Talmud, *Rosh Hashanah* 16b)

8. Rabbi Eliezer said: In Tishri the world was created, the patri-
archs (Abraham and Jacob) were born, the patriarchs died ... on
Rosh Hashanah, Sarah, Rachel, and Hannah were remembered; on
Rosh Hashanah, Joseph was released from prison; on Rosh Hashanah
before the exodus, the slavery of our ancestors in Egypt was ended.
(Talmud, *Rosh Hashanah* 10b–11a)

ROSH HASHANAH IN THE
PRE-SYNAGOGUE ERA

The attributes that we have come to associate with the first of
Tishri, those of a New Year and a Day of Judgment, are not
spelled out in the biblical verses that refer to Rosh Hashanah. The
biblical verse of Leviticus 23:24 describes Rosh Hashanah as a day
of rest and a memorial proclaimed by the blast of the shofar. In
Numbers 29:1, Rosh Hashanah is described as a holy convocation
and a day of sounding the shofar on which no work is to be
performed.

It is likely that the sacrificial rites of the first of Tishri were not
unique, inasmuch as similar rites were conducted on all festivals.
The only distinct ritual, unique to Rosh Hashanah, was the blast of
the shofar. The average Jew of antiquity was probably unimpressed
by this ritual because the Sanctuary regularly resounded to the
blasts of trumpets when the additional Musaf offering was sacrificed on the Sabbath and festivals. (Numbers 10:10)

Nonrabbinic sects, such as the Samaritans, the Sadducees, and
the Karaites, did not regard the first of Tishri either as a New
Year or as a Day of Judgment. Ancient Jews, particularly prior to
the Babylonian exile (sixth century B.C.E.) were hardly aware of the
significance of Rosh Hashanah. They may even have considered
the day a minor holiday. The only imposing holidays were the

pilgrimage festivals of Passover, Sukkot, and Shavuot, at which times the entire nation was enjoined to assemble in Jerusalem.

Rosh Hashanah, on the other hand, was mainly observed in the privacy of one's home. In the absence in those days of synagogues and a prescribed order of prayers, the sacrificial rite of Rosh Hashanah was confined to the Temple, and most of the people did not witness it. The same was true of the blowing of the shofar, which was done by the Kohanim, the Jewish Priests, in conjunction with the ritual of the Musaf additional offering.

The commandment to hear the sound of the shofar was not restricted to the Temple. (Talmud, *Rosh Hashanah* 33a) It is most unlikely, however, that in ancient times this ritual was observed outside of Jerusalem. Most people lacked the required skill, and there were no synagogues where a skilled person could blow the shofar in public.

When Ezra came to Jerusalem in 458 B.C.E. he discovered a community weakened by assimilation. He assembled the people on the first of Tishri and read to them passages from the Five Books of Moses. The assembly burst out crying a mood of contrition and penitence. Ezra comforted them: "This day is holy unto Adonai your God, neither mourn nor weep." (Nehemiah 8:9) The people were unaware of the nature of the day. He told them to go home "to eat the fat and drink the sweet, and send portions" to the poor. On the second day (possibly the second day of Rosh Hashanah according to the Jerusalem Talmud, *Eruvin*, Chapter 3, the holiday was celebrated for two days in Palestine since the time of the former prophets) the people were instructed to prepare for the festival of Sukkot. Once again, there was no mention of the blowing of the shofar on either day. Apparently this was omitted because the rite of the shofar had been performed in the Temple by the Kohanim.

AFTER THE ESTABLISHMENT OF THE SYNAGOGUE

The growing significance of the sound of the shofar began with the establishment of the synagogue in the period of the Second Temple. In Egypt, synagogues are known to have existed by 250 B.C.E., and the sounding of the shofar on the first of Tishri was unquestionably among the early rituals introduced into the synagogue, in addition to a prescribed order of prayers and the reading of the Torah. According to the Talmud, *Rosh Hashanah* 29b, even in the environs of Jerusalem people no longer depended upon the Temple rite of the shofar because the practice had spread to synagogues in their own locations.

Initially, the task of sounding the shofar was entrusted to the Jewish Priests, since they had also been in charge of this ritual in the Temple. In the talmudic account (*Rosh Hashanah* 29b) of a public fast for rain in the second century of the common era, selections of Rosh Hashanah prayers that preceded the sounding of the shofar were recited, and following that the Kohanim were requested to blow the shofar. As time passed, more and more Israelites acquired the skill of sounding the shofar. Others, according to the talmudic tractate of *Rosh Hashanah* 29b, brought the shofar to an expert.

The peak in the widespread practice of shofar blowing was reached after the destruction of the Temple in the year 70 C.E., when the synagogue became the primary institution of Jewish religious life. The matter of the rite and qualifications of the shofar was left to the jurisdiction of the Kohanim.

Rabban Gamaliel, the earliest rabbi to use the name Rosh Hashanah, assured the centrality of the shofar in the synagogal Rosh Hashanah service. By the second century C.E. we find the greatest number of rabbis involved in legal discussions pertaining to the shofar. This preoccupation attests to the pre-eminence of the shofar rite by the second century C.E.

By the time the existing practices of the Jewish people were organized and written down in the law code of the Mishneh (about 200 C.E.), the rabbis concluded that the new moon of Tishri is when God again is crowned the King and it is at this time that God passes judgment upon the world. In about the year 500 C.E., the rabbis brought together their own commentaries on the Mishneh into what then became known as the Talmud. By that time, the idea of obedience to God the King had been shaped into a powerful metaphor of the decent relationships that human beings owe each other. Thus the rabbis wrote (*Rosh Hashanah* 16b) that "one is judged on Rosh Hashanah, and one's doom is sealed on Yom Kippur, the Day of Atonement. Four things can avert the doom of a sinner: righteous deeds of kindness, prayerful supplication, change of name, and change of conduct."

The Talmud gives the metaphor of the Book of Life to Jewish tradition: "Three books are opened on Rosh Hashanah: one for the thoroughly wicked, one for the thoroughly righteous, and one for those in-between. The thoroughly righteous are immediately inscribed definitively in the Book of Life; the thoroughly wicked are immediately inscribed in the Book of Death; the destiny of those in-between is suspended from Rosh Hashanah until the Day of Atonement. If they do well, they are inscribed in the Book of Life; if they do not do well, they are inscribed in the Book of Death." (Talmud, *Rosh Hashanah* 16b)

Thus the Talmud creates an unbreakable bridge of the Ten Days from Rosh Hashanah to Yom Kippur. From talmudic times and onward, Jewish communities have celebrated Rosh Hashanah according to the Talmud's pattern. Of course, over the centuries the service has been enriched by many liturgical poems and various customs, such as Tashlich, in which bread crumbs that symbolize one's sins are cast into a body of river (which shall be discussed later in this volume). But the basic mood and intention have not changed.

SIX

ROSH HASHANAH : HOME
AND SYNAGOGUE OBSERVANCE

IN THE HOME

Rosh Hashanah falls on the first two days of Tishri, the month connected with the fall equinox. It will fall in September or October on the civil calendar. The calendar is arranged such that the first day of Rosh Hashanah is never allowed to fall on a Sunday, Wednesday, or Friday. This is done so that Yom Kippur, the Day of Atonement that comes ten days later, will never fall on a Friday or a Sunday—that is, immediately before or after the Sabbath, which would make for a most difficult transition. Reform Jews celebrate Rosh Hashanah for one day only, the first of Tishri. In Israel, however, it is celebrated for two days.

Rosh Hashanah, like all Jewish holy days, begins at sunset. At dusk on the first evening of the festival, families gather in their homes and recite the blessing over the candles and the blessing over the wine, known as the Kiddush. The challot are round, symbolizing God's crown, instead of the usual long shape. Many families taste a new fruit, often a pomegranate, and recite the Shehecheyanu blessing, thanking God for having allowed us to eat this new fruit and enabling us to reach this festive season. In addition, there is a custom to eat an apple dipped in honey, symbolizing the promise of a sweet new year.

Following are the basic blessings for the festival of Rosh Hashanah:

Festival *Kiddush*

בָּרוּךְ אַתָּה יהוה אֱלֹהֵינוּ מֶלֶךְ הָעוֹלָם, בּוֹרֵא פְּרִי הַגָּפֶן.
בָּרוּךְ אַתָּה יהוה אֱלֹהֵינוּ מֶלֶךְ הָעוֹלָם, אֲשֶׁר בָּחַר בָּנוּ מִכָּל עָם
וְרוֹמְמָנוּ מִכָּל לָשׁוֹן וְקִדְּשָׁנוּ בְּמִצְוֹתָיו. וַתִּתֶּן לָנוּ יהוה אֱלֹהֵינוּ
בְּאַהֲבָה אֶת (יוֹם הַשַּׁבָּת הַזֶּה וְ)אֶת יוֹם הַזִּכָּרוֹן הַזֶּה. יוֹם
(זִכְרוֹן) תְּרוּעָה (בְּאַהֲבָה) מִקְרָא קֹדֶשׁ זֵכֶר לִיצִיאַת מִצְרָיִם. כִּי
בָנוּ בָחַרְתָּ וְאוֹתָנוּ קִדַּשְׁתָּ מִכָּל הָעַמִּים. וּדְבָרְךָ אֱמֶת וְקַיָּם לָעַד.
בָּרוּךְ אַתָּה יהוה מֶלֶךְ עַל כָּל הָאָרֶץ מְקַדֵּשׁ (הַשַּׁבָּת וְ)יִשְׂרָאֵל
וְיוֹם הַזִּכָּרוֹן.

Barukh atah adonai eloheinu melekh ha'olam borei p'ri hagafen.
Barukh atah adonai melekh ha'olam asher bachar banu mikol am
v'rom'manu mikol lashon v'kid'shanu b'mitzvotav vatiten lanu adonai
eloheinu b'ahavah et yom (hashabbat hazeh v'et yom) hazikaron
hazeh yom (zikhron) t'ru'ah (b'ahavah) mikra kodesh zeicher litzi'at
mitzrayim ki vanu vacharta v'otanu kidashta mikol ha'amim ud'varkha
emet v'kayam la'ad. Barukh atah adonai m'kadeish (hashabbat v')
yisra'eil v'yom hazikaron.

Praised are You, Adonai, Sovereign of the Universe, who has chosen and distinguished us from all others by adding holiness to our lives with mitzvot. Lovingly you have given us the gift of (this Shabbat and) this Day of Remembrance, a day for (recalling) the sound of the shofar, a day of holy assembly recalling the exodus from Egypt. You have chosen us and endowed us with holiness from among all peoples. Your faithful word endures forever. Praised are You, Adonai, Sovereign of all the earth who hallows (Shabbat and) the people of Israel and the Day of Remembrance.

Shehecheyanu

בָּרוּךְ אַתָּה יהוה אֱלֹהֵינוּ מֶלֶךְ הָעוֹלָם, שֶׁהֶחֱיָנוּ וְקִיְּמָנוּ וְהִגִּיעָנוּ לַזְּמַן הַזֶּה.

Barukh atah adonai eloheinu melekh ha'olam shehecheyanu v'kiymanu v'higi'anu laz'man hazeh.

Praised are You, Adonai our God, Sovereign of the Universe, who has kept us alive, sustained us, and helped us to reach this moment.

On Dipping Apples in Honey

יְהִי רָצוֹן מִלְּפָנֶיךָ יְיָ, אֱלֹהֵינוּ וֵאלֹהֵי אֲבוֹתֵינוּ שֶׁתְּחַדֵּשׁ עָלֵינוּ שָׁנָה טוֹבָה וּמְתוּקָה.

Y'hi ratzon mil'fanecha adonai eloheinu veilohei avoteinu shet'chadeish aleinu shanah tovah um'tukah.

May it be Your will, Adonai our God and God of our ancestors, to renew for us a new, sweet, and good year.

בָּרוּךְ אַתָּה יהוה אֱלֹהֵינוּ מֶלֶךְ הָעוֹלָם, בּוֹרֵא פְּרִי הָעֵץ.

Barukh atah adonai eloheinu melekh ha'olam borei p'ri ha-etz

Praised are You, Adonai our God, Sovereign of the Universe, who creates of the fruit of the tree.

Candlelighting

בָּרוּךְ אַתָּה יהוה אֱלֹהֵנוּ מֶלֶךְ הָעוֹלָם, אֲשֶׁר קִדְּשָׁנוּ בְּמִצְוֹתָיו
וְצִוָּנוּ לְהַדְלִיק נֵר שֶׁל (שַׁבָּת וְשֶׁל) יוֹם טוֹב.

*Barukh atah adonai eloheinu melekh ha'olam asher kid'shanu
b'mitzvotav v'tzivanu l'hadlik neir (shabbat v'shel) shel yom tov.*

Praised are You, Adonai our God, Sovereign of the Universe, who
has made us holy by mitzvot and instructed us to kindle the festival candles.

ROSH HASHANAH GREETINGS AND FOODS

Most Jewish festivals have their own special greetings and foods.
For Rosh Hashanah, the traditional greeting is to wish another person a *shana tova*—good year; or the longer form of the greeting—*leshana tova teekatayvu*—"may you be inscribed for a good
year." One may also wish another a *chag sameach*—"happy holiday" or in Yiddish, *goot yuntoff*, which also means "good holiday."

Every festival has also assigned special foods as part of its celebration. For Rosh Hashanah, the main qualities of the special foods
are sweetness (for a sweet year), roundness (for the cycle of the
year), and abundance (for fruitfulness and prosperity). Special foods
for Rosh Hashanah would typically include *teiglach* (honey confec-
tions), honey cake, kreplach, fruitcake, and the like.

In some Jewish communities, the challot, the loaves of bread,
are baked in the form either of a ladder or a bird. The birdlike
challah is an allusion to the biblical passage: "As fluttering birds so
will the Lord of Hosts shield Jerusalem." (Isaiah 31:5) Those who
have the ladderlike challah take their cue from the character of
the day. On Rosh Hashanah man's destiny is determined: whether

he will live or die, whether he be poor or rich. Thus, on this day, life is likened to a ladder. A person will either ascend or descend, succeed or fail.

Fish is also a popular food for the night of Rosh Hashanah and when eating it some people have the custom of praying that their numbers increase as fish multiply.

Pomegranates often grace the Rosh Hashanah table. By eating them, one expresses the prayer and hope that on this Day of Judgment the Heavenly Court will find us filled with as many good deeds and accomplishments as the number of seeds in a pomegranate.

The types of vegetables that one eats on Rosh Hashanah are also significant. Peas are often eaten for the same reason as the pomegranate, because the Aramaic word for peas is *rubiya*, derived from *rav*, an "abundance." Dates and pumpkin dishes are also popular in some Jewish households, because of their sweetness.

On the other hand, nuts are often avoided on Rosh Hashanah, because the Hebrew word for them is *egoz*, the numerical value of which is the same as that of *chet* (the final aleph omitted), which means "sin."

IN THE SYNAGOGUE

Rosh Hashanah is primarily a synagogue-oriented festival. Services on this day are substantially longer than usual. The High Holy Day prayerbook used on Rosh Hashanah (and Yom Kippur, too) is called a *Machzor*, literally meaning "cycle." The book contains many of the prayers of both the daily and Sabbath service, in addition to special holiday liturgical poems, called *piyyutim*, which are the distinctive feature of the High Holy Day liturgy. These poems were composed in many lands during a period of about one thousand years, and reflect a passionate yearning for messianic redemption from exile, a steadfast faith in God's justice and mercy, a love for the Torah, and a firm belief in Israel as the vehicle of God's revelation to humankind.

The ark is opened and the congregation stands during the recitation of certain of these *piyyutim*, adding to the solemn atmosphere. The *Machzor* characterizes Rosh Hashanah as the birthday of the world, and continually reiterates the hope that people may unite to perform God's will with a perfect heart. Many of the prayers in the *Machzor* declare Rosh Hashanah to be a Day of Judgment on which the Ruler of the Universe summons all people before His Tribunal of Justice. In the heavenly Book of Records, the deeds of each person are inscribed and in that book is the seal of every person's hand.

The traditional Torah reading for the first day of Rosh Hashanah (Genesis 21) tells about the birth of Isaac to Abraham and Sarah. Tradition holds that on Rosh Hashanah Sarah gave birth to Isaac. The Torah reading for the second day of Rosh Hashanah (Genesis 22) tells of the difficult test to which Abraham was subjected when God told him to sacrifice his beloved son Isaac.

The Musaf additional prayers are divided into three parts: *Malchuyot* ("royalty"), which describes God as the Sovereign One; *Zichronot* ("remembrance"), which mentions the events that God remembers on Rosh Hashanah; and *Shofarot* ("sounding the ram's horn"), which recalls events connected with the shofar.

The solemnity of Rosh Hashanah is expressed in the liturgy. Not only the prayers, but the traditional melodies, help to create this special mood. Even the prayers that are not specifically designated for this festival are intoned to regal music whose melody is used only for the High Holy Days.

Many synagogues today hold several Rosh Hashanah services. In addition to the main service for adults (usually held in the synagogue's main sanctuary), there may be a service for preschoolers as well as one for teenagers. These services are especially designed to be engaging at the appropriate age levels and often afford opportunity for active participation.

TASHLICH : CASTING AWAY OUR SINS

The custom of symbolically casting the sins into a running brook on the first day of Rosh Hashanah following the *Mincha* afternoon service, presumably dates from the fourteenth century and is referred to as *Tashlich* ("you will cast"), a word borrowed from the Book of Micah 7:19 ("You will cast all our sins into the depths of the sea"). It is mentioned for the first time in *Sefer Maharil* by Rabbi Jacob Moellin, a leading fourteenth-century authority on Jewish customs and liturgy. He explains the custom of Tashlich as a reminder of the *Akedah* (binding), the attempted sacrifice of Isaac, concerning which Jewish legend relates that Satan, in an effort to prevent Abraham from fulfilling the divine command, transformed himself into a deep stream on the road leading to Mount Moriah. Plunging into the stream, Abraham and Isaac prayed for divine aid, whereupon the place became dry land again. A more rationalistic explanation suggests that *Tashlich* gives people a chance to reflect on water's purifying effect on the body and to be reminded that even as the body is purified by water, so ought their souls be purified by repentance and the appeal to God's help and mercy. The prayers recited at the *Tashlich* service are taken primarily from Micah 7:10–20, Psalm 118:5–9, and Psalms 33 and 130.

At the end of the *Tashlich* service participants throw breadcrumbs (symbolizing their sins) into the water as a symbol of their desire to cast away their sins and mend their ways.

According to some rabbinic authorities, the body of water into which the breadcrumbs are cast should contain fish. The precariousness of the existence of fish reminds people of their precarious existence and thus is intended to put them into the mood to repent.

There are numerous variations of *Tashlich* in countries throughout the world. For instance, in the Galician village of Bolehov the Hasidim would march to the river for Tashlich carrying lighted candles. They ignited small bundles of straw and placed these floating boats on the water. When darkness fell, there was the spectacular scene of fire and water on the river.

Jews of Kurdistan, as reported by the Jewish traveler Israel ben Joseph Benjamin, would jump into the river during their *Tashlich* service and cleanse themselves completely of their transgressions. In some Oriental Jewish communities *Tashlich* was recited in the synagogue around a basin of water into which live fish were placed.

There are also some new and interesting *Tashlich* customs that have been spotted in various communities in America. In one, members of the community sit in a circle with separate bowls of salty water and fresh, sweet water scattered around the circle. They sing *"Vetaher Leebaynu"*—purify us O God so that we may serve you in truth. Then, using pens of water-soluble ink, each of them write on a piece of paper some of their misdeeds of the past year.

Then the paper is thrown into the bowls of water, and participants watch their misdeeds dissolve. Following this, they turn to the bowls of fresh water, and as a way of showing that each one has accepted that all the others had confronted themselves and taken responsibility to change their lives, each person uses a cup to pour water from this bowl over the hands of the next person in the circle. This is followed by the singing of *"Oseh Shalom."*

Another custom at *Tashlich* services is the formation of a circle by the families attending the *Tashlich* service. Family members then ask and discuss questions such as: How would you evaluate this

past year? In what ways might each of us try to improve ourselves
during the coming year? What new mitzvot will we try to perform this year? At the end of the discussion, each family member
blesses the other, using a blessing formula such as the following:

May God bless you with _____ and _____. May
you be _____. May
this Rosh Hashanah of _____ (year) fill you with ____
_____.

SEVEN

SELECTED ROSH HASHANAH LAWS, CUSTOMS, OMENS, AND QUOTATIONS

The following laws and customs are culled, in the main, from important rabbinic sources, including the Code of Jewish Law, Judaism's most authoritative law code. This summary concentrates on those laws that relate to the individual.

NIGHT OF ROSH HASHANAH

1. It is customary for women to recite the blessing *shehecheyanu* prior to lighting the festival candles. In a situation where the same person who lights the candles recites the Kiddush over the wine (e.g., a man or woman living alone), the Shehecheyanu may be said only once, preferably after Kiddush. (*Shaarei Teshuvah* 263:4)

2. When praying the Amidah, several passages are interpolated from the first night of Rosh Hashanah until the end of Yom Kippur. In the first blessing the formula *zachrenu*, remember us, is added. In the second, *mee kamocha*, who is like You; in the second to last, *uchtov*—and inscribe. In the last blessing, *besefer*—in the book. The

ending of the third blessing of the Amidah—*ha-El hakadosh*—the holy God, is changed to *ha-Melech hakadosh*—the holy King, to accentuate God's role as Ruler and Judge of the world. (*Code of Jewish Law, Orach Chayim* 582:5)

3. It is customary to dip an apple into honey before eating one's meal. (*Code of Jewish Law,* condensed version, Laws of Rosh Hashanah)

4. Some people avoid eating nuts during this period because the Hebrew word for nut, *egoz,* has the same numerical value as *chet* (sin). Additionally, nuts cause an excessive flow of saliva and mucus to the mouth and may disturb a person's concentration on his prayers. (*Rama, Code of Jewish Law, Orach Chayim* 583:2)

5. It is customary not to eat sour or bitter things (e.g., sour pickles). (*Matteh Ephraim* 53:3)

6. Some have the custom of studying the four chapters of the Mishnah of Rosh Hashanah at the end of one's meal. (*Matteh Ephraim* 583:4)

7. After reciting the grace after the meal one should study Torah for a while before saying Shema and retiring for the night. (*Code of Jewish Law, Orach Chayim* 235:1)

ROSH HASHANAH DAY

1. One should be certain to recite the Shema within the first quarter of the day. (*Code of Jewish Law,* condensed version, *Laws of Shema*)

2. After the Amidah, the entire prayer Avinu Malkenu ("Our Father, Our King") is recited. (*Code of Jewish Law, Orach Chayim* 584)

3. In many synagogues it is customary to have a short recess before the sounding of the shofar. One should not spend the intervening time in idle chatter but try to utilize every precious minute of the Day of Judgment. Some people utilize this time to recite Psalms and study the laws of the shofar. (*Matteh Ephraim* 588:2)

SOUNDING THE SHOFAR

1. Two blessings are recited by the person blowing the shofar. The congregation fulfills its obligation to recite the blessings by listening and responding Amen. Therefore, it is of utmost importance to listen to every word and to intend to fulfill one's obligation thereby.

2. The one who sounds the shofar should stand erect during the blessings and the actual sounding of the shofar. Nowadays it is the custom for the entire congregation to stand when the shofar is blown. (*Code of Jewish Law, Orach Chayim* 585:1)

3. During the sounding of the shofar it is essential that one listen intently in order to hear every single shofar blast. (*Condensed Code of Jewish Law, Laws of the Shofar*)

4. From the recitation of the blessings until the last blasts have been completed at the end of Musaf, one may not speak about matters not concerning the blasts or the prayers. If one did speak after he had heard the *tekiah* blast, he need not recite the blessing again. However, if he spoke between *shevarim* and *teruah*—even concerning something relevant to the mitzvah—he should repeat that set of sounds [*tekiah, shevarim-teruah, tekiah*] later on. (*Code of Jewish Law, Orach Chayim* 592:3)

5. Women are not obligated by either biblical or rabbinic law to fulfill the mitzvah of the shofar. However, it is a universally ob-

served custom for them to observe the performance of this mitzvah. If a woman could not hear the shofar blasts in the synagogue she may blow the shofar herself. (*Code of Jewish Law, Orach Chayim* 589:6)

6. If a person is still in the middle of the silent *Amidah* when the shofar is about to be sounded, he may pause in the middle of his prayer and listen to the shofar blasts. (*Matteh Ephraim* 591:13)

OTHER ROSH HASHANAH LAWS

1. It is customary not to sleep at all during the daytime of Rosh Hashanah. (Rama, Code of Jewish Law, Orach Chayim 583:2) However, one who idles his time is considered as though he were sleeping. Chayei Adam says one should learn Torah after the meal, while it is customary in many communities to recite the entire book of Psalms. (*Matteh Ephraim* 598:1)

2. In the afternoon of the first day of Rosh Hashanah the *Tashlich* prayer is said at a body of water, preferably containing live fish. If the first day is on the Sabbath, *Tashlich* is postponed until the second day. (Code of Jewish Law, *Orach Chayim* 583:2)

3. There is a widespread custom to dip the challah in honey at the Rosh Hashanah meal as well as during all of the meals of Shabbat and *Yom Tov* until *Shemini Atzeret.* (cf. *Matteh Ephraim* 597:4)

4. Upon leaving the synagogue on Rosh Hashanah, we should walk leisurely, cheerful and confident that God has mercifully heard our prayers and the sounds of the shofar. We should eat and drink to the fullest extent of the bounty that God has bestowed upon us. Yet we must guard against eating to excess, as the fear of God must always be upon us. (*Condensed Code of Jewish Law, Laws of Rosh Hashanah,* 129:20)

SIGNIFICANT ROSH HASHANAH OMENS
AND SIGNS

The following is a cross-section of omens related to the festival of Rosh Hashanah:

1. The custom of eating symbolic foods on Rosh Hashanah is based on a Talmudic teaching (*Horayot* 12a). Abaye taught: Now that you have said that an omen is significant, each person should habituate himself to eat, at the beginning of the year, gourds, fenugreek, leeks, beets, and dates. Rashi, the medieval commentator, explains (Talmud, *Keritut* 6a) the symbolism of these five species in two ways. Some of them grow and ripen early and rapidly (and thus represent increased merits) while others are sweet-tasting and signify a sweet year.

2. Rabbi Z'vid taught: The first day of Rosh Hashanah, if it is hot, the entire year will be hot. If it is cold, the entire year will be cold. (Talmud, *Baba Batra* 147a)

3. There is an acceptable custom not to sleep during the daytime of Rosh Hashanah. The custom is based on the dictum of the Jerusalem Talmud: "If one sleeps at the beginning of the year, his guardian angel will sleep." (*Darchei Moshe*)

4. Rabbi Ammi said: One who wishes to ascertain whether he will live through the year or not should, during the ten days between Rosh Hashanah and Yom Kippur, kindle a lamp in a house where there is no draft. If the light continues to burn, he may be certain that he will live through the year. (Talmud, *Horayot* 12a)

5. The entire sustenance of man for the year is fixed for him from Rosh Hashanah to the Day of Atonement, except the expenditure for festivals and for the instruction of his children in the Law. If he

spent less for any of these he is given less and if he spent more, he is given more. (Talmud, *Betzah* 16a)

NOTABLE ROSH HASHANAH QUOTATIONS

1. Adam was created on Rosh Hashanah. He stood before His Judgment on the same day. He repented on the same day and God forgave him. (*Zohar* iii, 100b)

2. On Rosh Hashanah we should go about with a subdued spirit. (Talmud, *Rosh Hashanah* 26)

3. The angels asked God: "Why does Israel not chant the Hallel before You on Rosh Hashanah as on other holy days?" God replied: "The Books of Life and Death are open before Me on Rosh Hashanah. Shall I listen to Psalms of Praise?" (Talmud, *Arachin* 10)

4. A person awaiting trial is usually dejected, and wears somber garments. Israel, however, is different. On Rosh Hashanah the children of Israel dress in holiday clothes, and eat a festival meal. They are certain of God's mercies. (Jerusalem Talmud, *Rosh Hashanah* 1:3)

5. Rabbi Berechiah said: "It is the Creator's Will that on Rosh Hashanah the hearts of all people should be directed to God in unison." (Jerusalem Talmud, *Rosh Hashanah* 1:3)

6. It was on Rosh Hashanah, in the first hour of the day, that the thought came to God to create Adam, the world's first human being. (*Midrash, Leviticus Rabbah* 29:1)

7. On the New Year, Rachel and Channah were remembered on high. On the New Year, Joseph went forth from prison. On the New Year, the bondage of our ancestors in Egypt ceased. (Talmud, *Rosh Hashanah* 10b–11a)

8. Rabbi Judah says: "Man is judged on the New Year and his doom is sealed on the Day of Atonement." Rabbi Jose says: "Man is judged every day, as it says, 'And you visit him every morning'" [Job 7:18]. Rabbi Nathan says, "Man is judged every moment, as it says, 'You try him every moment'" [Job 7:18]. (Talmud, *Rosh Hashanah* 16a)

9. Rabbi Judah ben Ilai said: "The fate of everything in nature is under judgment on Rosh Hashanah, and is sealed on various days: the fate of grain on Passover, the fate of fruit of Shavuot, the fate of water on Sukkot; the fate of man, however, is sealed on Yom Kippur." (Talmud, *Rosh Hashanah* 16a)

10. All good things come to Israel through the shofar. They received the Torah with the sound of the shofar. They conquered in battle through the blast of the shofar. They are summoned to repent by the shofar, and they will be made aware of the Redeemer's advent through the great shofar. (*Eliyahu Zuta* 22)

11. When a person sins during the year, a record of his transgression is inscribed in faint ink. If that person repents during the Ten Days of Penitence, the record is erased. If not, it is rewritten in indelible ink. (*Otzar Midrashim*, p. 494)

12. The shofar sound of *tekiah* urges us to beg for God's mercies. The sound *teruah-shevarim* breaks the enslavement of our heart to desires. (*Sefer HaChinnuch*)

13. "Sound the shofar to the God of Jacob." Why not to the God of Abraham or Isaac? Because Abraham and Isaac were satisfied to have the Divine Presence rest upon a mountain and in a field; but Jacob foresaw a House of God as a place fitting for the Shechinah, and, when we assemble on Rosh Hashanah in a synagogue, we do so with Jacob's viewpoint. (*Pesikta Rabbati*, 40, 2)

14. As in the shofar, the voice goes in at one end, and comes out at the other, so will the words of the accuser enter God's ears and come forth again without leaving any influence. (*Peskita Rabbati*, 41, 6)

15. On Rosh Hashanah the bondage of the Jewish people ceased in the land of Egypt. (Talmud, *Rosh Hashanah* 11a)

17. The Sages said: "And God will say to Israel—yea—unto humanity too—'My children, I look upon you as if today, on Rosh Hashanah, you have been made for Me anew, as if today I created you, a new being, a new people, a new humanity.'" (*Midrash, Leviticus Rabbah*, 29:10)

ROSH HASHANAH GLOSSARY

The following are the terms basic to an understanding of the festival of Rosh Hashanah.

Avinu Malkeinu: "Our Father, Our King." Well-known High Holy Day prayer.

High Holy Days: Rosh Hashanah and Yom Kippur.

L'shanah tovah tikateivu: "May you be inscribed for a new year."

Machzor: Festival prayerbook.

Malchuyot: "Royalty." The first of the three divisions of the Musaf Additional Service on Rosh Hashanah.

Musaf: The special additional service.

Rosh Hashanah: "Head of the year."

Shabbat Shuvah: "Sabbath of Repentance." The Sabbath between Rosh Hashanah and Yom Kippur.

Shofar: Ram's horn sounded on Rosh Hashanah.

Shofarot: "Sounding of the shofar." The third of the three divisions of the Rosh Hashanah Musaf Additional Service.

Shevarim: Three blasts of the shofar.

Selichot: Prayers of forgiveness recited during the High Holy Days.

Tashlich: A Rosh Hashanah afternoon service, which takes place beside a flowing stream or river. Here bread crumbs, symbolizing one's sins, are cast in the water.

Ten Days of Repentance: The ten-day period starting on Rosh Hashanah and ending on Yom Kippur. Also called the Days of Awe.

Tishri: The seventh month of the Hebrew year, the first of which is Rosh Hashanah.

Tekiah: One long blast of the shofar.

Tekiah Gedolah: One very long blast of the shofar.

Teruah: Nine quick staccato notes of the shofar.

Yom HaDin: "Day of Judgment." Another name for Rosh Hashanah.

Yom HaZikaron: "Day of Remembrance." Another name for Rosh Hashanah.

EIGHT

ROSH HASHANAH IN SHORT STORY

A ROSH HASHANAH PARABLE

This little story emphasizes the importance of doing things on time, and not postponing them for a later time. With regard to the High Holy Days, it is not simply enough to think about changing our bad habits and ways, and making promises to do so. We have to act upon our promises as soon as possible. Our thoughts must lead us to action!

Once upon a time there was a poor woman who had many children. Her children were always hungry, forever begging their mother for food. One day she found an egg.

She called her children together and said, "Children, you have nothing to worry about any more. I have found this egg. Being a careful woman, I will ask my neighbor for his hen so that this egg will be hatched. When the egg hatches a chick, though, we'll wait for it to grow up so it can lay more eggs. Eventually we will have more chickens and many more eggs. But we still won't eat the eggs. I will sell them to buy a nice cow. But we won't eat the cow, for I shall sell the cow to buy a large field, and we won't need anything anymore!" Suddenly, the egg fell out of the woman's hand and it broke.

This is how we are. When Rosh Hashanah comes, we all promise to change our ways, thinking "I will do this" and "I will do that." But the days slip by and our thought does not lead us to action. Therefore we must all be careful that our thoughts lead us to action.

THE FIREMAN

This story reminds us of one of the purposes of the blowing of the shofar. The sounds of the shofar are meant to awaken the Jewish people to change their ways and improve themselves. It is not enough simply to listen to the sounds of the shofar and think that we have finished our duty to God. We must be certain that the sounds of the shofar arouse us to action. We must change our ways and improve our behavior in order for the shofar sounds to have fulfilled their duty.

A long time ago most houses were made out of wood and there were no such things as fire engines or electric fire alarms. When a fire erupted, a whole town could go up in flames. So when a fire broke out, all the townspeople would leave their businesses to help put it out. There used to be a watchtower that was taller than the other buildings. A watchman kept a lookout all the time. As soon as he saw a fire, he would sound the alarm, and the people would move into action.

Once it happened that a young boy from a small village came to town for the first time. He stopped at an inn outside the town and heard the sound of the bugle. He asked the innkeeper what this meant.

"Whenever we have a fire," the innkeeper explained, "we sound the bugle and the fire is quickly put out."

"How terrific!" thought the boy. "What a surprise I will bring to my own village."

The boy went out and bought himself a bugle. He called all of the villagers in his town together and said, "You will never have to be afraid of a fire anymore. Just watch and see how quickly I can put out any fire."

Saying this, he ran to the nearest house and set fire to its wooden roof. The fire began to spread very quickly.

"Don't be alarmed!" cried the boy. "Now just watch me."

The boy began to blow the bugle with all his might. But the fire did not seem to care too much for the bugle sounds. Soon all of the houses in the village were on fire.

The villagers now began to scold the boy. "You fool," they cried. "Did you think that the mere sounding of the bugle would put out the fire? It is only the call of an alarm, to wake up the people, if they are asleep, or to break them away from their business and send them to the well to draw water for the fire."

ALEF, BET, GIMEL, DALET

The theme of this story is the importance of praying with proper intention. True prayer is saying things honestly and truthfully, with your whole heart and soul. Merely saying words with no feeling is not enough. This story can be read responsively, thus making it very experiential. Each time the reader completes a paragraph, have everyone chant aloud, "Alef, Bet, Gimel, Dalet."

Reader: It was Rosh Hashanah. Everybody had come to synagogue to welcome the new year and pray for good things in the coming year. Suddenly there was some noise in the back of the sanctuary.

Everyone: Alef, Bet, Gimel, Dalet.

Reader: Everyone became very quiet. And then from the back of the room they heard it again.

Everyone: Alef, Bet, Gimel, Dalet.

Reader: One by one, people began to turn and look to see the person who was interrupting the service. Sitting at the back of the sanctuary was a young boy. He was standing with his prayerbook open, saying over and over again:

Everyone: Alef, Bet, Gimel, Dalet.

Reader: Soon, the rabbi stopped his prayers. He too was looking at the boy who said over and over again:

Everyone: Alef, Bet, Gimel, Dalet.

Reader: Suddenly, the boy stopped looking at his mahzor and began to cry. He said, "I can't read Hebrew. All I know is how to say the first four letters of the Hebrew alphabet. I kept saying them over again, hoping that God would turn them into a prayer."

The rabbi of the congregation then kissed the boy and said: "Today we have learned the real meaning of prayer. Prayer is opening our hearts to God and saying things honestly. Then the rabbi announced: "Let us pray together." And everyone in the sanctuary joined in:

Everyone: Alef, Bet, Gimel, Dalet.

A ROSH HASHANAH TALE

This little folktale reminds us of the importance of looking carefully at ourselves and our deeds. Before we put ourselves in order

and improve ourselves, we need to remind ourselves of the things
we did wrong over the past year. This is the real purpose of
prayer, especially on Rosh Hashanah and Yom Kippur.

Once there was a man who sat in study before Rabbi Mordecai
of Nadvorna. Before Rosh Hashanah he came to obtain permission
to be dismissed. The rabbi said, "Why are you hurrying?"

The man answered, "I am a prayer leader, and I must look at
the festival prayerbook and put my prayers in order."

The rabbi answered, "The prayerbook is exactly the same as it
was last year. But it would be much better if you were to look
inside yourself, and put your deeds in order."

TOGETHER WE LOOK FOR A
NEW WAY

In this story we learn that when two people find themselves spiri-
tually lost and on the wrong path in life, they must cooperate
and look for the way out and the right path together. The theme
of community responsibility is an important one for the High Holy
Days.

Once our master Rabbi Chayim of Zans told this parable: A
man had been wandering in a forest for several days, not knowing
how to get out. When he saw another person approaching he
became very excited and said to himself, "I will surely find out
which is the right way." When the two got close to each other,
he asked the man, "Brother, tell me which is the right way."

The other man answered, "I do not know the way out either.
I have been wandering in this forest for many days too. But this
much I can tell you. Do not take the way I have been taking, for
that will lead you on the wrong path. Let us look for a new way
out together."

Rabbi Chayim added, "So it is with all of us. One thing I can tell you. The way we have been following is not the right way. Let us now look for a new way together."

POPE ELHANAN

Once a son was born to Rabbi Simeon the Great of Mayence, whom they named Elhanan. One Sabbath a Gentile woman came in to tend the stove, and she saw little Elhanan playing with his nurse, for his parents were away at synagogue. She picked up the boy and took him out of the house. The nurse said nothing, for she thought that the woman wished only to play with the child for a while. But when she did not return, the nurse became alarmed and went in search of the child. But she could find no trace anywhere of the woman or the child.

When the parents returned from synagogue, she told them what had happened, and they too searched the city but to no avail. The child was gone. So they tore their clothes and wept.

The Gentile woman took the child that she had stolen to a monastery, where he was raised as a Christian. Because of his sharp and inquisitive mind, he became a great scholar and eventually rose to the position of cardinal in Rome. When the old Pope died, Elhanan was named the new Pope.

But all this time, he knew that he had been born a Jew. Yet, because of the honors and riches he had acquired in his new faith, he could not bring himself to return to the faith of his ancestors.

Now the desire grew in him to see his father, Rabbi Simeon. So he thought of a scheme to force his father to come to him in Rome. He issued a papal decree forbidding the Jews of Mayence to circumcise their sons, to keep the Sabbath, or to immerse themselves in the ritual bath. He thought, "They will send their greatest leaders to ask me to annul my decree. Surely Rabbi Simeon will be at their head."

And so it came to pass. The Jews of Mayence were devastated by the Pope's decree, so they appealed to the bishop of the city to have it repealed. But the bishop said to them, "This order comes from the Pope himself. I am powerless to undo it."

So they sent a delegation to Rome. At its head, as Elhanan had predicted, was Rabbi Simeon. They came to the Jewish community of Rome and told them what had happened.

"How odd," said the Roman Jews when they heard of it, "for this Pope has always been such a good friend to the Jews. Daily he converses with Jewish scholars, plays chess with Jews, seeks their wisdom. What have you done to bring God's wrath down upon your heads through this Gentile?"

They declared a fast and gave much charity to avert the evil decree.

Then they went to the cardinal and asked him to speak to the Pope on behalf of the Jews of Mayence.

"I cannot," said the cardinal, "for it was his idea alone to issue this decree. You must go to him yourself."

So the delegation went to St. Peter's and asked for an audience with the Pope.

"I wish to see only the leader of the delegation!" declared the Pope.

Rabbi Simeon came in and saw the Pope playing chess. The son recognized the father, but the father did not recognize the son. Then the Pope began to converse with Rabbi Simeon on all manner of topics. Rabbi Simeon was amazed at the range of his knowledge. He knew as much about Jewish books and philosophy as any Jewish scholar. Then they sat down to play chess. Although Rabbi Simeon was the best chess player in Mayence, the Pope easily beat him. In every way the Pope's mind surpassed his own.

Then the Pope sent everyone away so that they could be alone.

"Father, do you not recognize me?" he cried, and he began to weep.

"How would I recognize your holiness?" asked Rabbi Simeon. "I have never before been to Rome."

"Did you not lose your young son when a Gentile woman carried him off on a Sabbath?" said the Pope. "I am that son!"

Rabbi Simeon was astonished to hear his words and did not believe them.

"It is true, Father," continued the Pope. "I am your son who was lost to you all these years. I have never forgotten who I am and have longed to return to the faith of my birth."

"Return then, my son," said Rabbi Simeon. "Blessed is God who redeems the captive!"

The Pope's face darkened. "Long have I known that I was a Jew, but I could not bring myself to give up the comforts of this life. Will God forgive me?"

"Repentance awaits all those who turn back," answered Rabbi Simeon. "God will show mercy to anyone who opens up his heart."

"Go home in peace, Father," said the Pope, "and show the letters I will give you to the bishop. He will annul my decree. Tell no one what you have heard today. I must first do something here, and then I will come to you in Mayence."

So Rabbi Simeon returned to Mayence and gave the Pope's letters to the bishop. The Jews of the city rejoiced greatly to have the Pope's harsh decree annulled.

As he had promised, Rabbi Simeon told no one about his son except his wife, who rejoiced greatly to learn that he was still alive. In Rome, the Pope wrote a letter against his adopted faith and left it with instructions that it was to be read by all his successors. Then he fled Rome in disguise, came to Mayence, and resumed the faith of his parents. He became an even greater scholar than before, and his fame spread throughout the Jewish world.

In gratitude for his son's return, Rabbi Simeon wrote a hymn of praise for the Second Day of the New Year. In it he included the phrase: "God has shown grace"—Elhanan.

RABBI AMNON OF MAYENCE

Rabbi Amnon, the leader of the Jews of Mayence, was a wealthy and handsome man of good family. The bishop of the city wished to convert him, so he sent messengers to him day after day. One day, when Amnon had grown tired of their endless arguments, he said to them, "Give me three days to consider what you have said."

As soon as they had gone, Amnon was stricken with shame. How could he have had any doubts about his faith?

In three days the bishop sent for Amnon, but he refused to come. So the bishop had him brought against his will.

"What is your answer?" asked the bishop.

"I will sentence myself," declared Amnon. "Let the tongue that expressed doubt be cut out!"

"No," said the bishop, "your tongue shall not be cut out, for it spoke the truth. Rather your legs and hands, which refused to obey me, shall be cut off."

So they cut off his hands and feet and poured salt in his wounds. As they cut off each joint, the bishop asked him if he was ready to convert. "No!" he said each time, so they sent him home with his severed members beside him.

Then the people knew that he was truly worthy of his name, Amnon—"a man of faith."

On Rosh Hashanah, he asked to be taken to the synagogue. There he composed the Unetah Tokef prayer, which he recited to all assembled: "We acclaim this day's pure holiness, its awesome power ... The great shofar is sounded. A still, small voice is heard ... 'The day of judgment is here!'"

Then he died. Three days later he appeared to Rabbi Kalonymus ben Meshullam in a dream and taught him the entire hymn, ordering him to teach it to Jews throughout the Diaspora.

But others say he died in Cologne. Just before he died, he instructed his students to take him back to Mayence and bury him beside his ancestors there.

"It is too dangerous!" they told him.

"Then prepare my body for burial, lay my coffin in a ship, and set it afloat on the Rhine."

When he died, they did as he had instructed them.

Without pilot or crew, the ship traveled upstream against the current and arrived in Mayence. When the Christians tried to seize hold of the ship, it leapt backward out of their hands.

But when the Jews of the city gathered on the shore, the ship neared them and did not leap away. They boarded the ship and found a letter: "My brothers and sisters in the holy community of Mayence, I have departed this world and ask that you bury me by the graves of my ancestors. Peace be with you!"

But when the Jews tried to remove the coffin and bring it to the Jewish cemetery, the townspeople attacked them and tried to steal the coffin. But it stayed where it was and could not be lifted. So the townspeople built a church above it. No matter how much money the Jews offered for the coffin, the leaders of the city would not turn it over.

Then one night several young Jews went outside the city and took a hanged man down from the gallows, dressed him in a white shroud, and exchanged his body for that of Rabbi Amnon's. Then they buried Amnon beside the graves of his family, and there he rests in peace to this day.

TWO SOCKS ON ONE FOOT

Once there was a man who used to sin without remorse. On Rosh Hashanah every year, at the time of Tashlich, he would take his sins to the lake in a sack and cast them away. Then he would go back to his sinning.

Now this man and his wife, who was a saintly woman, had no children. So they came to the Baal Shem Tov and asked him to intercede for a child. Because of his wife's good deeds, the Baal Shem Tov agreed to do so. A year later the woman bore a healthy baby boy.

With a heart full of joy, the man returned to the Baal Shem Tov to thank him for his help. But the Baal Shem Tov only shook his head sadly when the man stood before him.

"Your son's life is in mortal danger because of your sins," he warned him. "When your son reaches the age of bar mitzvah, he will go to the lake and drown, for the lake is angry with you, since you have blackened its waters with so much sin."

"Is there no way to save him?" cried the anguished father.

"If you keep him away from the water on his thirteenth birthday, the curse will be annulled."

"This we will surely do!" cried the man.

"It is not as easy as that," cautioned the Baal Shem Tov. "Thirteen years is a long time. By the time your son reaches the age of bar mitzvah, you will have forgotten all that I have told you. But God will send you a reminder: On the day your son puts two socks on the same foot, that day your son must not go near the water or he will surely die!"

The man thanked the rabbi for his advice and hurried home to tell his wife.

The years passed and the son grew to be a handsome, learned, and pious boy, the apple of his parents' eye. In time the parents forgot all about the Baal Shem Tov's dire prediction, for the boy was strong and healthy and seemed safe from all harm.

But on the day of his thirteenth birthday, he rose early and began to dress, and by accident put two socks on the same foot. He came to his mother and asked her for the missing sock. Suddenly terror seized her heart, for she remembered what the Baal Shem Tov had told them thirteen years before.

She ran to tell her husband, and together they locked the boy in his room. No matter how loudly he protested, they refused to let him out. That day was an especially hot summer's day, and the boy cried out bitterly for a glass of water. But even that they would not give him. Finally, he fell asleep on his bed, exhausted and forlorn.

As the sun began to set, a ghostly hand rose out of the lake, followed by a second hand, and then a head. The last of the bathers looked on in horror as the head slowly gazed along the shore, apparently looking for something.

Then an angry voice burst forth, "One is missing!"

Moments later the head slowly sank back into the swirling black waters from which it had emerged.

And so the boy was saved from a terrible death, and the father from the path of sin.

BEGIN WITH YOURSELF

When Hayyim of Zanz was a young man, he set about trying to reform his country from its evil ways. But when he reached the age of thirty, he looked around and saw that evil remained in the world. So he said, "Perhaps I was too ambitious. I will begin with my province." But at the age of forty his province too remained mired in evil. So he said, "I was still too ambitious. From now on I will only try to lift up my community." But at fifty he saw that his community had still not changed. So he decided only to reform his own family. But when he looked around, he saw that his family had grown and moved away, and that he now remained alone.

"Now I understand that I needed to begin with myself."

So he spent the rest of his life perfecting his own soul.

NINE

TEN DAYS OF REPENTANCE

The ten days between Rosh Hashanah and Yom Kippur are known as the days of penitence, beginning on the first of the Hebrew month Tishri and ending with the close of Yom Kippur. According to rabbinic tradition, three books are opened on New Year's Day: the righteous are inscribed for life, the wicked for death, while the intermediate remain in suspense until the Day of Atonement. By means of good works and repentance they can make the swaying balance incline in their favor, that they may live. (Talmud, *Rosh Hashanah* 16b).

These ten days of repentance between Rosh Hashanah and Yom Kippur are designated as *yamim noraim*—solemn days in the Jewish calendar, marked by contrition and prayers for divine forgiveness, and a turning away from the pettiness of our daily life. During this time, Jewish people take special care to give to charity, to avoid gossip, and to be helpful to others.

These days remind Jews that they are in a sense suspended between two days of judgment—between Rosh Hashanah, when one's judgment is inscribed, and Yom Kippur, when it is sealed. One who possesses this awareness is less likely to turn his or her thoughts away from the fear of judgment and the obligation of repentance.

Maimonides explains that while prayer and repentance are pleasing to God at any time, God finds them especially pleasing during the Ten Days of Repentance.

During these ten days additional prayers are recited. Special selichot penitential prayers are said before dawn by traditional Jews, and great care is generally exercised in the observance of mitzvot. During this period too, the wording in the prayer service is somewhat changed. For instance, the word l'eila (higher) is repeated during the Kaddish prayer, and thus is recited l'eila u'leila (higher and higher). The year-round wording alludes to the exaltation of God beyond all earthly blessing. The usage for the ten days of repentance speaks of an even greater divine exaltation. Also, during the Amidah prayer, we ask that God "remember us and inscribe us in His Book of Life." In the prayer Magen Avot (shield of our ancestors), which follows the Amidah on Friday evening, the words hamelech hakadosh (Holy King) are said instead of the usual ha'el Hakadosh (the Holy God). In addition, the prayer Avinu Malkeinu (our Father and King) is recited during the morning daily service

SHABBAT SHUVAH (SABBATH OF REPENTANCE)

The Sabbath between Rosh Hashanah and Yom Kippur is designated as Shabbat Shuvah—the Sabbath of Repentance. It is called the Sabbath of Repentance because the Haftarah of that morning begins in Hebrew with the words shuvah yisrael—return Israel. (Hosea 14:2) Besides its special Haftarah, the Sabbath of Repentance is marked in some synagogues by a traditional lengthy discourse about repentance. In Eastern Europe, rabbis spoke only twice a year in the synagogue—on the Sabbath of Repentance and on *Shabbat HaGadol* before Passover.

FAST OF *GEDALIAH*

Immediately after Rosh Hashanah, the third day of Tishri, is the observance of a fast day in commemoration of the murder of Gedaliah, the Jewish governor appointed by King Nebuchadnezzar over the poor of the land after the destruction of Jerusalem in 586 B.C.E. He was treacherously assassinated at his residence by Ishmael of the royal dynasty. Gedaliah shared the views of the Prophet Jeremiah with regard to yielding to the Babylonians and serving them.

In Jeremiah 38:17, the prophet's message to King Zedekiah reads: "if you surrender to the officers of Babylon's king, you shall save your life; this city shall not be destroyed with fire, and you and your family shall live. But if you do not surrender to the officer of Babylon's king, this city shall fall into the hands of the Chaldeans, who shall destroy it with fire, and you shall not escape their hands."

Gedaliah adjured the people, after the Babylonian conquest of Jerusalem, not to be afraid to serve the Chaldeans, to stay in the land and submit to the King of Babylon, for their own welfare. (Jeremiah 40:9–10) After the assassination, Gedaliah's followers fled to Egypt for fear of the king's revenge,

The fast of Gedaliah thus commemorates a tragic event, which completed the destruction of the First Commonwealth of Israel.

TEN

YOM KIPPUR

*On the tenth day of the seventh month is the day of atonement;
you shall have a holy convocation and you shall afflict your souls—*
Leviticus 23:27

BACKGROUND

Yom Kippur, the Day of Atonement, has one basic focus: to encourage people to do their part in repairing the world by repairing
themselves. Jewish mystics believe that God actually descends
through the spheres of heaven in order to dwell among the people
during Yom Kippur. It is at this time, say the mystics, that God is
the most accessible. Hence, one appears before God, the Judge of
all humanity, in order to atone for the sins of the previous year
and commit oneself to better one's life. But first one must ask for
forgiveness of those one has wronged. Thus we are taught that
"Yom Kippur atones for transgressions against God, but it does not
atone for transgression of one human being against another unless
we have made peace with one another." (Mishnah, *Yoma* 8:9)

YOM KIPPUR IN THE BIBLE

The biblical name for the fast of the tenth of Tishri is *Yom KaKippurim*. (Leviticus 23:27) No explanation is given in the Bible for the timing of Yom Kippur. It is neither an agricultural nor a commemorative day. According to the Bible (Leviticus 16:29–31; 23:27–32; Numbers 29:7), all manner of work is forbidden on the day of Atonement and the soul is to be "afflicted." Special sacrificial offerings were also to be brought and a ceremony with a great deal of pageantry was already in existence in biblical times. Here are excerpts of the description of the ceremony of the so-called "Avodah" ceremony as described in Leviticus 16:1–34:

> God spoke to Moses: "Speak to Aaron your brother, that he come not at all times into the holy place within the veil, before the ark cover which is upon the ark; that he die not. For I appear in the cloud upon the ark cover. Herewith shall Aaron come into the holy place: with a young bullock for a sin-offering, and a ram for a burnt offering. He shall put on the holy linen tunic, and he shall have the linen breeches upon his flesh . . . he shall bathe his flesh in water. And he shall take of the congregation of the children of Israel two he-goats for a sin-offering, and one ram for a burnt offering. And Aaron shall present the bullock of the sin offering, which is for himself, and make atonement for himself, and for his house. And he shall take the two goats, and set them before God at the door of the tent of meeting. And Aaron shall cast lots upon the two goats: one lot for God, and the other lot for Azazel. And Aaron shall present the goat upon which the lot fell for God, and offer him for a sin-offering. But the goat, on which the lot fell for Azazel, shall be set alive before God, to make atonement over him, to send him away for Azazel into the wilderness. And Aaron shall present the bullock of the sin offering, which is for himself, and shall make atonement for himself,

and for his house, and shall kill the bullock of the sin offering which is for himself. And he shall take a censer full of coals of fire from off the altar before God, and his hands full of sweet incense, and bring it within the veil. And he shall put the incense upon the fire before God, and the Cloud of the incense may cover the ark cover that is upon the testimony, that he die not. And he shall take the blood of the bullock, and sprinkle it with his finger upon the ark cover on the east, and before the ark cover shall he sprinkle of the blood with his finger seven times. Then shall he kill the goat of the sin offering, that is for the people, and bring his blood as he did with the blood of the bullock, and sprinkle it upon the ark cover. And he shall make atonement for the holy place, because of the uncleanness of the children of Israel, and because of their transgressions, even all their sins. . . . And there shall be no man in the tent of meeting when he goes in to make atonement in the holy place, until he come out, and have made atonement for himself, and for his household, and for all the assembly of Israel. And he shall go out to the altar and make atonement for it. . . . And when he has made an end of the atoning for the holy place, and the tent of meeting, and the altar, he shall present the live goat. And Aaron shall lay both his hands upon the head of the live goat, and confess over him all the trans-gressions of the children of Israel. . . . And he shall put them upon the head of the goat, and shall send him away by the hand of an appointed man into the wilderness. And the goat shall bear upon him all their iniquities unto a land which is cut off. . . . And he shall then bathe his flesh in water in a holy place, and put on his other vestments and come forth and offer his burnt offering and the burnt offering of the people, and make atonement for himself and for the people. . . . And it shall be a statute forever unto you. In the seventh month, on the tenth day of the month, you shall afflict your souls and shall do no manner of work, the home-born, or the stranger that sojourns among you. For on this day shall atonement be made for you, to cleanse you, from all your sins shall you be clean before God. It is a sabbath or solemn rest for you, and you shall afflict your souls. It is a statute forever.... And he shall make atonement for the most holy place, and he shall make atonement for the tent of meeting and for the altar; and he shall make atonement for the priests and for the people of the assembly. And this shall be an everlasting statute for you, to make atonement for the children of Israel, because of all their sins once in the year."

From this description we can see the example of vicarious atonement by which the High Priest placed his two hands on the goat to be sent away, and thereby having confessed, symbolically transferred the people's sins to the head of the animal. In this way the souls of the people were purified of their transgressions.

Theodore Gaster, a noted historian of Jewish ceremonies, points out that a public purgation of the accumulated communal sinfulness is to be found in a variety of cultures. In ancient Babylon, for example, the rite of *kuppuru*—purgation—came in the midst of the ten-day coronation festival, and involved the sacrificing of a ram in order to eliminate impurity in holy places. In addition, there was a public confession of sins by the king, followed by a human scapegoat—a condemned criminal—that was publicly beaten in the streets.

THE DAY OF ATONEMENT DURING TEMPLE TIMES

The ritual performed by the High Priest in the Jerusalem Temple was the central feature of the Day Atonement and conformed to the instructions in the Bible. The High Priest placed his hands on the bullock and confessed his sins and those of his household. Subsequently a second confession was made for the Kohanim, and thereafter two goats were brought before him. One was sacrificed, and the other was sent off into the desert with the symbolic load of the sins of the Israelites.

It is speculated that despite the rich pageantry and colorful vestments of the High Priests that the impact of Yom Kippur on preexilic Jewry was not profound. Since it was not one of the three pilgrimage festivals, Yom Kippur likely did not attract large crowds to Jerusalem.

The Yom Kippur pageantry in the Second Temple is well documented in the Talmud. In addition to the biblical rituals previously cited, the Talmud describes some rituals not mentioned in the Bible. One of these was the recitation of a short prayer by the High Priest when he left the sanctuary (Talmud, *Yoma* 53a): "May it be your will... that no exile shall come upon us... and if exile shall come upon us... may we be exiled to a place of Torah. May it be your will that this year be a year when prices are low, a year of plenty, a year of rain, and that your people Israel may not need one another's help... and that they do not rise to rule over one another. (Jerusalem Talmud, *Yoma* 5).

Another innovation was the public reading by the High Priest of Torah portions pertaining to Yom Kippur. The procedure in the tractate *Yoma* 68a is described as follows:

The *chazan* handed the Torah to the head of the synagogue who turned it over to the deputy priest, who in turn transferred it to the High Priest.

The Talmud (*Yoma* 35b, 41b) also preserves the text of the High Priest's three confessions on Yom Kippur.

Rabbi Ishmael described another Yom Kippur ritual performed in the Temple: A thread of crimson wool was tied to the door of the sanctuary. When the Azazel goat reached the wilderness and the rite was completed, the thread turned white. This was a providential sign that the sins of Israel had been forgiven. (Talmud, *Yoma* 68b).

The Talmud *Yoma* 19b also describes the special efforts that were made to keep the High Priest awake during the night of Yom Kippur.

The custom of immersion was also introduced in the Second Temple period. We are told that the High Priest would immerse himself five times (Talmud, *Yoma* 19b), and from this custom derived the post-talmudic custom of immersing in a mikveh on the eve of the Day of Atonement.

According to the sages, the goat dispatched to the wilderness as part of the Temple ritual on the Day of Atonement atones for all transgressions, (Talmud, *Shevuot* 1:6), whereas after the destruction of the Temple the Day itself atones. (*Sifra, Acharei Mot* 8:1) However, most of the sages were of the opinion that even the atonement of the goat was only effective for one who repented, for the Day of Atonement only atones when accompanied by repentance. (Talmud, *Yoma* 8:8–9) This is the source of the custom of asking forgiveness of one another on the eve of the Day of Atonement.

No definitive knowledge is available about the Day of Atonement prayers during the period of the Second Temple. According to the philosopher Philo, it was already customary during these times to spend the whole day, from morning to evening, in prayer.

Once the Temple had been destroyed and the sacrificial system abolished, the rabbis concluded that the Day of Atonement must be a day on which people ask for forgiveness from their transgressions—those between people and those between themselves and God. The biblical affliction of one's soul on this day was interpreted for all time to mean (Talmud, *Yoma* 8:1): fasting from food, from drinking water, from washing or anointing the body, from wearing leather shoes (a sign of luxury), and from sexual intercourse. The same kinds of work are forbidden on Yom Kippur as are forbidden on the holy Sabbath.

ELEVEN

YOM KIPPUR HOME AND SYNAGOGUE OBSERVANCES

While Jewish holidays are traditionally observed for two days in the Diaspora (except in Reform synagogues), Yom Kippur is exempt. The observance of a two-day fast would be an undue hardship. While the specific timing of Yom Kippur is determined by Rosh Hashanah, it does not occur on a Saturday evening since one cannot prepare for Yom Kippur on the holy Sabbath.

Since Yom Kippur is to be a "sabbath of complete rest," the laws of the Sabbath are also enacted on Yom Kippur. Beyond this, as previously noted, the rabbis understood self-denial to refer to fasting and a prohibition against wearing leather sandals, anointing the body with oils (cosmetics), bathing for pleasure, and the enjoyment of sexual relations with one's spouse.

IN THE SYNAGOGUE

Services are convened as a court with the Divine Judge sitting in judgment. Normally one may not pray in the company of sinners, but in this context permission to do so is publicly given, since all are sinners coming to admit their sin as a community of individuals.

Evening services begin with the chanting of *Kol Nidrei* ("all our vows"), a prayer that asks God to absolve one of all bonds and oaths. This prayer is chanted three times by the cantor. According to one opinion, this is done in order to assure that latecomers may hear it at least once. A more cogent suggestion is that in the case of the absolution of vows, which *Kol Nidrei* actually is, the absolution has to be said three times. (Code of Jewish Law, *Yoreh Deah*, 228:3) The *Amidah*, the confessional, and a series of penitential *piyyutim* are also recited during the Kol Nidrei evening service.

In the morning service the cantor actually rises from the midst of the congregation in order to truly be its *shaliach tzibbur* ("messenger").

Yom Kippur is one of the few occasions during which the worshipper stays in the synagogue throughout the day. Confessional prayers are offered. The synagogue ark and Torah are adorned in white covers, as are the rabbi and cantor in their white robes. Some congregants wear white as well to symbolize atonement and purity. A tallit is worn beginning with the evening *Kol Nidrei* service and continues to be worn throughout the entire next day through the conclusion of the service. The *Kol Nidrei* service must be recited before darkness begins, since according to Jewish jurisprudence no court may issue a verdict at night. If the improvised court, standing with the Torah scrolls are to release the congregation from all vows, this must be done while it is still day.

Other salient aspects of synagogue observance include a litany of forty-two sins at the heart of the confessional. As they are recited, worshippers beat their breasts in contrition. One reason given for this custom is that by so doing a person addresses his heart with the accusation "You are the cause of the sin." (*Aruch HaShulchan* 607, par. 8)

After the *shacharit* morning service two Torah scrolls are removed from the ark: one for the section in the Book of Leviticus (16:1–34) dealing with the confessional service of the High Priest on Yom Kippur; and the second scroll (Numbers 29:7), which deals with the additional sacrifice (Musaf) of the day. Finally, the prophetic portion (Isaiah 57:14–58:14) deals with the true purpose of fasting. A fast is of no avail, says the prophet, if it does not induce a just and merciful relation with our fellowmen. (The Conservative movement, in a project called "Operation Isaiah," invites congregants to bring nonperishable food to the synagogue on Yom Kippur, in order to feed the hungry as it says in the Haftarah. After the holy day, the food is delivered to a local food bank.)

After the Torah and Haftarah readings the Yizkor memorial prayers are recited for the departed. This is followed by the Musaf Additional Service, which consists of a number of liturgical poems dealing with the theme of God as King, the recitation of the *Avodah* service describing the High Priest confessing sins, and the martyrology service recording the death of ten rabbis who died for the sanctification of God's name.

The *Mincha* afternoon service consists of a scriptural reading from Leviticus 18. It is a condemnation of adultery and other immoralities, and is a constant reminder to the worshipper that Yom Kippur is a time to be wholesome in mind and pure in heart, and that a high standard of domestic fidelity is the basis of a happy home life. The Haftarah for the afternoon is the reading of the entire Book of Jonah, which was chosen because it illustrates the power of repentance and shows that it is impossible to escape the presence of God.

The *Neila* service is the last of the five services of Yom Kippur. The name *Neila* ("closing") is derived either from the closing of the Temple gate, which took place around this time of day, or from the symbolic closing of the gates of heaven at the end of Yom Kippur. The *Neila* service thus assumes the character of a final appeal that the twenty-four-hour day of self-deprivation and prayer now coming to a close should have its atoning affect. Samson Raphael Hirsch views *Neila* as a recapitulation of the Divine service of the heart to which the entire day has been devoted, and of the message which one must now take with them when they seek to serve God through the activities of day-to-day living. (*Horeb,* no. 657) During the repetition of the *Amidah* prayer during the *Neila* service, the ark is kept open. Keeping the ark open gives visible expression to the fundamental plea of *Neila*: "Open for us the gates of Heaven at the time when the portals close." At the conclusion of the *Amidah* the *Avinu Malkeinu* ("Our Father, Our King") is recited, which provides the final moment of judgment as one pleads for mercy.

The Day of Atonement concludes with the sounding of the shofar, which marks the end of the fast. It has been suggested that the shofar is sounded at this point in memory of the Jubilee Year. In Temple times the beginning of the Jubilee was announced on the tenth day of Tishri (Yom Kippur), but since the reckoning of the fifty-year Jubilee cycle is no longer certain, it is done every year. Louis Ginzberg, professor of Bible at the Jewish Theological Seminary of America, saw this practice of sounding the shofar as an instance of the tendency to preserve vivid reminders of the Temple ritual in the Yom Kippur liturgy. In Temple times, the conclusion of every Yom Kippur, and of every Sabbath as well, was marked by the sounding of the shofar, and this practice was continued even after the Temple was destroyed. After the shofar

is sounded, worshippers say "*leshanah haba'ah beyerushalayim*"—
next year in Jerusalem.

At the conclusion of worship services, people go to their home or
to someone's home to which they were invited to break the fast.
They break the fast joyously, since according to legend, at the
close of Yom Kippur a heavenly voice proclaims: "Go your way,
eat your bread with joy, and drink your wine with a merry heart;
for God has already accepted your works." (Midrash, *Ecclesiastes
Rabbah* 9:7)

IN THE HOME

Of the many ways of preparing for the fast of Yom Kippur and
for the opportunity to make atonement for sins, perhaps the most
colorful is the ceremony of *kapparot* (atonement). In this ceremony,
now observed in traditional circles only, a chicken (or a fish or
even money) is swirled around the head of a child while these
words are spoken: "This is in exchange for you. This is in place of
you. But you will go to a good, long life and to peace." The chicken
is then taken to a kosher slaughterer and given to the poor as
tzedakah.

The afternoon before Yom Kippur was traditionally a time to
visit the mikveh, the ritual bathhouse, for an immersion that would
symbolize atonement and purification.

The meal before Yom Kippur itself (called in Hebrew the *seudah
mafseket*—separation meal) often consists of bread that is baked in
a winglike mold. This is to signify the concept that the intense
spiritual mood of Yom Kippur makes the Jews resemble angels with
wings. Others decorate the challah with a ladder, echoing the prayer
"let our entreaties climb to You." In some communities after dinner
the table would be covered with a fine tablecloth and books of

Torah spread upon it, to show that for Yom Kippur the words of prayer and study were replacing food.

Before going to services, a memorial candle is traditionally lit in memory of the departed members of the family. While the Kiddush over the wine is not recited at the start of Yom Kippur, a special candlelighting blessing is said:

בָּרוּךְ אַתָּה יהוה אֱלֹהֵינוּ מֶלֶךְ הָעוֹלָם, אֲשֶׁר קִדְּשָׁנוּ בְּמִצְוֹתָיו וְצִוָּנוּ לְהַדְלִיק נֵר שֶׁל (שַׁבָּת וְשֶׁל) יוֹם הַכִּפּוּרִים.

Barukh atah adonai eloheinu melekh ha'olam, asher kid'shanu b'mitzvotav v'tzivanu l'hadlik neir shel (shabbat v'shel) yom hakippurim.

Praised are You, Adonai our God, Sovereign of the Universe, who has made us holy by mitzvot and instructed us to light the (Shabbat and) Yom Kippur candles.

בָּרוּךְ אַתָּה יהוה אֱלֹהֵינוּ מֶלֶךְ הָעוֹלָם, שֶׁהֶחֱיָנוּ וְקִיְּמָנוּ וְהִגִּיעָנוּ לַזְּמַן הַזֶּה.

Barukh atah adonai eloheinu melekh ha'olam shehecheyanu v'kiymanu v'higi'anu laz'man hazeh.

Praised are You, Sovereign of the Universe, who has kept us alive, sustained us, and helped us to reach this moment.

Children are also traditionally blessed by their parents during the final meal before Yom Kippur.

TWELVE

SELECTED LAWS, CUSTOMS, AND QUOTATIONS FOR YOM KIPPUR

F ollowing are selected laws and customs related to the festival of Yom Kippur as culled from the *Code of Jewish Law*, condensed version.

THE DAY BEFORE YOM KIPPUR

1. On the day before Yom Kippur, it is customary to perform the ceremony of *kapparot*, at dawn, for the attribute of mercy is predominant at that time. Men select roosters and women select hens, while a pregnant woman takes both a rooster and a hen. . . . It is preferable to choose white fowl, with due attention to the biblical verse: "If your sins are red as the scarlet thread, they will become white as snow. ". . . Each takes the fowl in his or her right hand, recites the verses *"bene adam"* (children of man), and then swings the fowl around the head three times, each time reciting: *"zeh or zot chalifati"* (this is instead of you), but one must first swing it around his own head, and then above the head of the other.

It is also preferable that the fowl should be slaughtered at dawn. By no means should we imagine that the fowl atones for us, but we should reflect that what is done to the fowl should properly be done to us because of our sins.... Some people are accustomed to give the *kappara* fowl to the poor; it is best to redeem the fowl with money and give the money to the poor.

2. It is mandatory to feast sumptuously on the day before Yom Kippur, and the person who does it for the purpose of fulfilling this precept, is credited with having fasted also on that day. It is fitting to eat fish at the first meal.

3. Yom Kippur does not atone for transgressions committed against a fellow man unless we conciliate him, for it is written [Leviticus 16:30]: "For on this day God shall atone you of all your sins, you shall be cleaned before God," which means that only sins against God shall be atoned on Yom Kippur, but not sins committed against our neighbor, unless we conciliate him.... It is our duty to go personally to them. If, however, it is difficult for us to do so, or if we understand that they will be easily reconciled even if approached by another, we may conciliate them through a mediator. The person whose forgiveness is sought should grant forgiveness willingly and wholeheartedly, and not be obstinate.... Even if one has been grievously wronged, one should not seek vengeance, nor bear a grudge against the one that had wronged him. On the contrary, if the offender does not come to him to beg forgiveness, the offended person should present himself to the offender in order that the latter might ask his pardon. If a person harbors enmity in his heart, his prayers on Yom Kippur will not be accepted, God forbid; but the one who is magnanimous and forgiving, will have all his sins forgiven.

4. If the offended has since died, the offender should assembled ten men at the grave and say: "I have sinned against the God of Israel and against this man (so and so)" and they pronounce three times: "You are forgiven...."

5. Every man is duty bound to immerse on the day before Yom Kippur, to cleanse himself from nocturnal pollution, and also as a prerequisite to repentance, just as a convert to Judaism is required to immerse.... The most appropriate time for the bath of purification is after midday.

6. In accordance with the custom, every householder prepares two candles, one for the house, symbolizing the Torah, which is called "light" because on Yom Kippur, Moses descended from Mount Sinai with the second tablets and the other candle is for the souls of his departed father and mother, to make atonement for them. In pursuance to custom, the candle lit in the house burns till the following night, and is used for the havdalah light.

7. The *al chet* confessional prayer is recited while standing and in a bowed posture. At the mention of each sin, we beat our breasts as if to say: "You were the cause of my sins."

8. Toward evening, we eat the final meal before the fast, at which it is customary to dip in honey the piece of challah over which the *hamotzi* has been pronounced, as we do on Rosh Hashanah. Only food that is easily digestible should be eaten at this meal, such as the flesh of fowl.... One should not partake of food or drink that tend to generate heat, such as victuals seasoned with spices and saffron. We must be exceedingly careful to add from the profane to the sacred, that is, we should conclude the meal while it is yet day, a little before twilight. The zealous are prompt to end their meal amount an hour before nightfall. If we finish the meal long before sunset and we intend to eat or drink after that, we must make a declaration, or at least have it in mind, before reciting Grace after meals, that we do not yet inaugurate the fast.

9. It is the custom to put on a *kittle* (white robe), which resembles shrouds. It is calculated to humble the arrogant heart of man. A mourner may also put it on.

10. It is the custom of fathers and mothers to bless their children before going to synagogue on Yom Kippur, because the holiness of the day has already begun and the gates of mercy are already open. They implore in the blessing that the children should be granted good life and that their hearts be constant in the fear of God.

YOM KIPPUR EVE

1. It is the custom in our regions before saying *Kol Nidrei* that the most venerable man of the congregation takes out a Torah scroll from the Holy Ark, and walks with it around the center platform, while the people lovingly kiss it, and plead for pardon and forgiveness for having slighted it.

2. Some people stand on their feet during the evening service and also the whole day of Yom Kippur. If they feel faint, they may lean against something. The reason for standing is to simulate angels.

3. Some people stay in the synagogue all night reciting hymns. When in need of sleep, they must remove far from the Holy Ark. The cantor should not stay awake, as he may thereby weaken his voice.

YOM KIPPUR

1. It is forbidden to eat, drink, bathe, anoint, wear shoes, or have sexual intercourse on Yom Kippur. It is also forbidden to do any sort of manual labor, nor should one carry anything from one place to another, even as on the Sabbath.

2. Some authorities forbid, while others allow, touching either food or drink when it is necessary to feed a minor therewith. If possible, it is well to adhere to the stricter opinion.

3. Only washing for pleasure is forbidden on Yom Kippur. But even when permissible, one should be careful not to wash more than it is actually necessary.

4. All those who may eat on Yom Kippur, because of possible danger, may be given forbidden food, if permitted food is not available.

5. Children less than nine years old should not be permitted to fast even if they want to fast only a part of the day, because it may affect their health. Children nine years old and in good health should be trained to fast a little. They should abstain from food a few hours beyond their regular eating time.

6. On Yom Kippur, memorial prayers for the dead are said, because thinking of the departed saddens and humbles a person's heart.

7. The time for the beginning of the *Neila* concluding service is when the sun is over the tree tops, so that we may conclude it when the stars become visible.

8. On the conclusion of Yom Kippur we eat, drink, and rejoice. For it is stated in the Midrash (Ecclesiastes 9): "On the conclusion of Yom Kippur a heavenly voice goes forth and says: 'Go, eat your bread with joy, and drink with a merry heart your wine, for God has already accepted your deeds favorably.' "

NOTABLE YOM KIPPUR QUOTATIONS

1. Things between you and God are forgiven on Yom Kippur. Things between you and your fellow person are not forgiven, until he has forgiven you. (*Sifra* to *Acharei Mot*)

2. Satan accuses the Jews every day of the year except on the Day of Atonement. (Talmud, *Yoma* 20a)

3. Of the 365 days in the year, the Only One of the Universe had already designated one of them as His very own. Rabbi Levi said that it was the Day of Atonement. (*Pesikta Rabbati* 23:1)

4. If a person says, "I shall sin and then repent," he is given no opportunity to repent. If one says, "I shall sin and the Day of Atonement will atone," the Day of Atonement does not atone. (Talmud, *Avot de Rabbi Natan* 40:10)

5. The Holy Blessed One said to Israel: "Remake yourselves by repentance during the ten days between New Year's Day and the Day of Atonement, and on the Day of Atonement I will hold you guiltless, regarding you as a newly made creature. (*Peskita Rabbati*)

6. Just as if a nut falls into some dirt you can take it up and wipe it and rinse and wash it and it is restored to its former condition and is fit for eating, so however much Israel may be defiled with iniquities all the rest of the year, when the Day of Atonement comes, it makes atonement for them, as it is written, "For on this day shall atonement be made for you, to cleanse you." [Leviticus 16:30] (*Midrash, Song of Songs Rabbah* 6:11)

7. The merit of a fast day lies in the charity dispensed. (Talmud, Berachot 6b)

8. This was the prayer of the High Priest when he departed in peace from the sanctuary on Yom Kippur:

> May it be Your will, O God and God of our ancestors, that exile shall not be our lot, neither on this day nor in this year. But if exile be decreed for us either today or this year, let our exile be to a place where Torah is studied. May it be Your will, O God, and God of our ancestors, that we have no deficiency, neither on this day nor in this year. But if a deficiency be decreed for us either today or this year, let it be a deficiency caused by the performance of good deeds. May it be Your will, O God and God of our ancestors, that this year be a year of plenty, of trade, of rain, warm weather, and dew, and that Your people Israel will not be dependent upon one another. [Jerusalem Talmud, Yoma 5:3]

GLOSSARY OF YOM KIPPUR TERMS

Azazel: The place beyond the wilderness frontier to which the scapegoat was sent, burdened by the sins of the community.

G'mar chatimah tovah: Literally, "may you be sealed well (in the Book of Life)," greeting used from the end of Rosh Hashanah until the end of Yom Kippur.

Kol Nidrei: "All vows," prayer that annuls all promises from one Yom Kippur to the next. As a leitmotif it sets the tone at the beginning of the Yom Kippur service.

Neila: The final service of Yom Kippur. The word reflects the notion that the gates of the Temple were about to be closed at this time of day (and thus the opportunity to repent and change the decree was about to expire).

Selichot: Prayers of contrition, which along with confessionals color the day.

Shluggin kapporos: Yiddish name for the ceremony in which one twirls a chicken (or fish or money) around one's head in order to project one's sins into it and sent it to its death rather than the individual for his or her sins.

Tzom: Hebrew for fast.

Yoma: Fifth tractate of the order Moed (Festivals) of the Talmud, a part of which includes laws governing the observance of Yom Kippur.

Yom Hakippurim: Full Hebrew name for the holy day.

Yom Kippur Katan: "Minor Yom Kippur." The eve of each new month, which became a day of fasting and repentance for the very pious.

THIRTEEN

YOM KIPPUR IN SHORT STORY

A SIMPLE SHEPHERD'S MELODY

This story reminds us of the importance of saying our prayers with proper feeling and intention (kavanah). It is not simply enough to say words, nor are words the only way to communicate with God. Prayer is service of the heart, and speaking to God with true feeling is the best way to pray.

It was the day of Yom Kippur. All day long the Chasidim said their prayers for repentance, asking God for forgiveness. It was evening and time for the last of the Yom Kippur services, called Neila. The Chasidim were looking forward to finishing their prayers and going home to eat. But the Baal Shem Tov would not begin the Neila service.

At the same time a shepherd boy sat with his flocks. He knew that it was Yom Kippur, but he didn't know any Hebrew or prayers. He began to speak and said, "God, I know it's Yom Kippur and I know that I should pray to you. But I don't know the prayers and

I don't know Hebrew, so what I have to offer you tonight is the best I can do. I am sure you will understand me." And the boy took out his flute and played a melody.

At that exact moment in the synagogue the Baal Shem Tov began the Neila service. That evening, when everyone in the town broke the fast together, the Hasidim asked their rabbi. "Why did you wait so long to begin Neila? Hadn't we prayed loud enough all day? And then, why did you begin so suddenly?"

The Baal Shem Tov answered, "I had a vision that the gates of the heavens were closed and God had not yet accepted our prayers. Our prayers were like dust on the floor of the synagogue. They were not the service of the heart. They were just meaningless words, repeated just to be done with them. I could not end the Yom Kippur prayers because they would not be accepted. But all of a sudden I had a vision about a little shepherd boy who played the flute. And that flute song was real prayer, and when God heard it, God opened the gates of heaven to accept all of our prayers."

So we see that there are other ways to pray aside from just using the prayerbook. The important thing is that the prayers be real service of the heart.

A MOTHER'S PRAYERBOOK

It once happened that the Gentile lord of a village took a liking to a Jewish couple within his domain. When the old couple passed away, the lord adopted their only son, making the boy heir to all he possessed. In time the lord told the boy that his parents had been Jews, and he gave him the few poor possessions his parents had owned, among them his mother's prayerbook.

One year at the beginning of the Days of Awe, the boy saw all the Jews of the village walking to synagogue, and he asked them where they were going.

"We are going to ask God to inscribe us in the Book of Life," they told him. "For our fate will soon be decided for the coming year. God will certainly not reject our prayers."

From that moment on, the boy's heart began to turn toward God.

That night, his parents appeared to him in a dream, urging him to return to the faith of his people. Every night during the Ten Days of Penitence, the dream returned, and the boy's soul began to thirst for repentance. He told all this to the lord, but the lord only dismissed it as a phantom of the boy's imagination.

On the eve of Yom Kippur, the boy saw all the Jews of the village again making their way toward the synagogue, dressed in white, prayerbooks in their hands. He asked them what they were doing.

"We are seeking pardon for our sins," they told him, "On this day the Gates of Forgiveness are opened and God grants atonement."

Ignited by their words, the boy seized his mother's prayerbook and hurried to the synagogue, where he found all the people praying and confessing their sins. But he did not know how to pray, and he wept bitterly. And his cries stirred the heavens.

Brokenhearted, he rushed up to the bimah and placed his mother's prayerbook on the lectern. Then he gazed up toward heaven and declared, "Holy God! I do not know how to pray. I do not even know what to say. So here is the whole prayerbook!"

And his heart opened itself up to the spirit of repentance, and his prayer was accepted as that of a righteous soul. From that day on, he lived a life of perfect faith.

A CRYING BABY

On the eve of Yom Kippur, the entire congregation of Rabbi Moses Leib of Sassov gathered together in the synagogue to pray. But when the time came for Kol Nidre, the rabbi had still not arrived. They waited and waited, and finally decided to begin the Kol Nidre prayers without him.

Just then the rabbi rushed in, out of breath.

"Forgive me, good people," he said, "but on my way to synagogue tonight, I passed a house where I heard a baby crying. Her mother had already gone to synagogue, so I picked up the child and comforted her and then came here as fast as I could."

Then he began chanting Kol Nidre, and the angels rejoiced.

FOURTEEN

THE PRAYERS OF THE
HIGH HOLY DAYS

THE *MACHZOR*

The prayerbook is designated by two Hebrew words: *siddur*—order of prayers, and *machzor,* the literal meaning of which is "cycle." The former connotes a prayerbook for year-round use in synagogue and home. The latter contains the standard prayers of the siddur in addition to the additional liturgical poems (*piyyutim* in Hebrew), which are distinctive to the festivals. Though a High Holy Day prayerbook contains only part of the "cycle" of liturgies, it is nonetheless referred to as a *Machzor.*

The High Holy Day *Machzor* service comprises prayers created in the days of the Temple; liturgical poems dating from the Middle Ages; and other selections from the Bible, Talmud, Midrash, and medieval Jewish literature. The dominating and recurring theme throughout the book is God as Sovereign of the Universe.

This chapter presents selections from the *Machzor.* After each prayer is presented in the translation, it will be followed by a brief commentary related to the origin and background and main concepts.

ROSH HASHANAH PRAYERS

Avinu Malkeinu (Our Father, Our King)

Our Father, our King, we have sinned before you.

Our Father, our King, we have no king except You.

Our Father, our King, deal with us kindly for the sake of Your name.

Our Father, our King, renew for us a year of good.

Our Father, our King, annul the designs of those who hate us.

Our Father, our King, frustrate the counsel of our enemies.

Our Father, our King, destroy the power of every oppressor and enemy.

Our Father, our King, silence the mouths of our enemies and those who falsely accuse us.

Our Father, our King, remove pestilence, sword, famine, captivity, destruction, and plague from the children who obey Your covenant.

Our Father, our King, withhold the plague from your people.

Our Father, our King, forgive and pardon our iniquities.

Our Father, our King, blot out our transgressions, and cause our sins to pass away from before You.

Our Father, our King, erase in Your great mercy all record of our guilt.

Our Father, our King, may we return to You in complete repentance.

Our Father, our King, send a complete healing to the sick among Your people.

Our Father, our King, repeal the evil sentence decreed against us.

Our Father, our King, remember us for our well being.

Our Father, our King, write us into the book of happy life.

Our Father, our King, inscribe us in the book of freedom and salvation.

Our Father, our King, inscribe us in the book of sustenance.

Our Father, our King, inscribe us for a meritorious life.

Our Father, our King, inscribe us in the book of forgiveness and reconciliation.

Our Father, our King, cause salvation to quickly spring forth for us.

Our Father, our King, bring glory to Israel, Your people.

Our Father, our King, exalt the majesty of Your anointed redeemer.

Our Father, our King, provide us with abundant blessings.

Our Father, our King, fill our store houses with abundance.

Our Father, our King, hear our voice and take pity and have compassion on us.

Our Father, our King, receive our prayer with merciful favor.

Our Father, our King, open the gates of heaven to our prayer.

Our Father, our King, do not turn us away unanswered.

Our Father, our King, remember our fragility for we are but dust.

Our Father, our King, let this hour be an hour of mercy and a time of favor before You.

Our Father, our King, have mercy on us and upon our children.

Our Father, our King, do this for the sake of those who were killed for Your holy name.

Our Father, our King, do this for the sake of those who were killed for Your unity.

Our Father, our King, do this for the sake of those who went through fire and water for the sanctification of Your name.

Our Father, our King, bring to judgment those who have shed the blood of Your people.

Our Father, our King, grant our supplication for Your sake, if not for ours.

Our Father, our King, accept our prayer for Your sake and save us.

Our Father, our King, do this for the sake of Your abundant mercies.

Our Father, our King, do it for the sake of Your great and revered name.

Our Father, our King, be gracious to us and answer, for we are unworthy; deal with us in charity and kindness and save us.

Commentary

Avinu Malkenu is a prayer consisting of a series of invocations and supplications recited in the synagogue during the ten-day period of the High Holy Days and on fast days. It is mentioned in the Talmud (*Taanit* 25b) as the improvised prayer of Rabbi Akiva on the occasion of a drought.

The nucleus of five lines with the initial refrain *"Avinu Malkenu"* quoted in the Talmud, was in the course of time increased to forty-four lines. The phrases "our Father" and "our King" are borrowed from Isaiah 33:22; 63:16; 64:7, where God is addressed in such terms as these: "The Lord is our King, He will save us; You, O God, are our Father."

According to some commentators the litany *Avinu Malkenu* originally consisted of nineteen verses to correspond in contents and order to the nineteen benedictions of the *Amidah* prayer. This would explain why the prayer is recited after the *Amidah*. It is omitted on Sabbaths because the rabbis discouraged making personal requests to God on this holy day.

It has also been said that *Avinu Malkenu* on Rosh Hashanah and Yom Kippur takes the place of the Hallel service. The explanation, as given in the Talmud (*Berachot* 32b), is that on the days of judgment it is more fitting to recite supplications than hymns of praise and thanksgiving.

Finally, *Avinu Malkenu* reflects the frequent persecutions which have given rise to outcries such as: "Our Father, our King, abolish all evil decrees . . . rid us of every oppressor . . . remove pestilence, famine, and destruction from your people."

Melech Azur Gevurah
(O King, Girt with power)

O God, girt with power. Your name is great in strength. Yours is the arm of triumph. O King, dressed in garments of judgment, on the day of retribution, You will requite the evil of Your enemies. O King, dressed in splendor, You did dry up the sea, subduing the fury of the mighty waters.

The King is dressed in tenfold garments adorned in holiness to reveal the commandments of Israel. God is all powerful, and in the assembly of the holy ones, God is holy.

The King, who dwells in light, who as with a garment is robed in light, will bring forth our judgment into light. The King is surrounded with strength, mighty is God's right hand. Let mortal man not act presumptuously. You, O King, robed in righteousness and sanctified through righteousness, unto You, O God, belongs righteousness. . . .

The King mightily rules the world, and at God's majesty the mountains quake. They skip like rams at God's rebuke. The King, before whom all the Kings of the earth stand in awe, before whom the earth trembles and shakes, dwells above the cherubim. The King, whose majestic power none can restrain, who sustains all by His might, gives strength to the tired. . . .

The King, whose gaze shakes the earth's foundation, comprehends all things. The King scrutinizes all living creatures everywhere. The King of the universe. God is proclaimed Sovereign by His eternal people. "God shall reign forever." He is the Holy God.

Commentary

This *piyyut* was composed by Eleazar Kalir, one of the earliest medieval Hebrew poets, believed to have lived in the seventh or eighth century of the common era. Chanted on the first day of Rosh Hashanah, it envisions God as Sovereign both over nature and humankind. God is not only all powerful, but God is righteous and totally just. Because of God's justice, He will judge all people equitably, treading down the transgressors. For the worshipper, the poem reaffirms one's faith that the forces of wickedness will always be overcome by God.

It has been said that the idea of the ten garments of God is derived from a passage in the *Pesikta de Rav Kahana*. In that passage, God is portrayed in a variety of roles. They include destroying the corrupt generation of the flood, giving the Torah to the Israelites and decreeing the doom of the Babylonians. In this legendary description of the unfolding of history, God is metaphorically portrayed as wearing a garment of a different color on each occasion.

Melech Amon Ma'amarcha
(*O King, Your word stands steadfast*)

O King, Your word stands steadfast from long ago. Your name abides in glory with Your congregation; "Your word, O God, endures forever."

O King, on this day You finished Your work and from stern judgment You delivered man fashioned in Your image; for "from generation to generation is Your faithfulness."

O King, for his offspring You have decreed redemption so that through righteousness they may be worthy of Your love. "This day they stand at the bar of Your judgment."

They guard Your laws; they are Your witnesses, Your worshippers. O bear with them and exalt them that they may spread Your presence, "for they are Your servants. . ."

The season is come to sound the ram's horn, and thus recall Abraham's offering of "the ram which was caught by its horns in the thicket."

As the horn sounded at Sinai, the camp of Israel in awe stood afar off. All Merciful, remember this and be gracious to us in judgment; for lo, "the horn grew louder and louder. . ."

The King judges all nations with equity that He may be exalted, and from God's lofty height He regards and examines their cause. "God has established His throne with justice."

The omnipotent King is hallowed in righteousness. The Eternal is exalted and glorious in judgment; "God is ready to reward His servant with justice."

According to God's promise the King will temper His displeasure with mercy. God is nigh to justify the people that daily proclaim the unity of God's name; "God sustains His people Israel, every day."

Commentary

This *piyyut* was composed by Rabbi Simon ben Isaac ben Abun of Mayence in the eleventh century. Its content was drawn from a legendary homily on the Torah portion that opens with the verse "Forever O God Your words stand fast in heaven, Your faithfulness is unto all generations." [Psalm 119:89] On this verse Rabbi Eliezer comments that the world was created on the twenty-fifth day of

Elul, and on the first of Tishri, man was created. Thus, Rosh Hashanah is the birthday of humanity.

The theme of this *piyyut* is that every person is given a chance to win divine pardon and that God is a merciful God in judgment.

Zachrenu Lechayim
(Remember Us Unto Life)

Remember us unto life, O King who delights in life, and inscribe us in the Book of Life so that we may live worthily for Your sake, O God of life.

Commentary

Judaism has always emphasized the importance of life as a gift from God. The Book of Deuteronomy states: "Choose life, so that you may live." In this prayer, added to the *Amidah* during the ten days of Rosh Hashanah through Yom Kippur, the worshipper petitions God to remember him or her in life and to be inscribed in God's Book of Life.

The prayer itself is of uncertain age. The metaphor of a book of life can be seen in the statement found in the *Ethics of the Fathers* 2:1: Know what is above you—a seeing eye and a hearing ear, and all your deeds are written in a book. These three things prevent a person from transgression.

Attah Hu Elohenu
(You Are Our God)

You are our God in heaven and earth.
Mighty and powerful, acclaimed by throngs.
God spoke and it was, God commanded and it was created.
God's memorial is eternal, God lives forever.

God is all seeing, God dwells even in secret places.
God's crown is salvation, God's garment is righteousness.
God's robe is zeal, God is filled with justice.
God's secret is righteousness, God's counsel is faithfulness.
God's work is truth, God is righteous and just.
God is near to them that call on him in truth.
God is high and exalted.
God abides in the heavens, God suspends the earth in space.
O living and enduring, revered exalted and holy God.

Commentary

This alphabetical acrostic, originally the fourth part of Eliezer Kalir's liturgical poem for the New Year, celebrates the majesty, glory, and grandeur of God. The theology of the poem includes the attributes of God as all-seeing and all-powerful and all-holy. God is also close to all that call upon him truthfully.

Melech Elyon (King on High)

God who dwells on high, austerely mighty,
Shall eternally reign supreme.
God who keeps His word and probes hidden things,
Shall eternally reign supreme.
God who is all righteous and listens to prayer
Shall forever reign supreme.
God who helps children against the enemy
Shall forever reign supreme.
God, eternally good, who spreads the skies
Shall eternally reign supreme.
God robed in light, powerful and revered,
Shall eternally reign supreme.
God, Sovereign of all worlds, piercer of secrets,

Shall forever reign supreme.
God who sustains everything, survives all, sees all,
Shall eternally reign supreme.
God, glorious and mighty Redeemer,
Shall eternally reign supreme.
God, near to all who call on Him with love,
Shall eternally reign supreme.
God, who never sleeps, whose heavens are peaceful,
Shall eternally reign supreme.
Mortal king decays and descends to the grave,
Tired and restless; how long shall this one reign?
Mortal king is overcome by deep sleep,
Struck by things of vanity; how long shall this one reign?
God eternal in power, glory and reputation,
Shall eternally reign supreme.

Commentary

The author of this *piyyut* is not known. Structurally, it is a threefold alphabetical acrostic, which recounts God's eternal majesty and power. Its main concepts include the fact that God is dependable and reliable, infinite in power, and near to all those who seek God's help. This is in sharp contradistinction to an ordinary human king upon which people depend. Compared to God, mortal kings are relatively powerless.

L'El Orech Din (God Who Orders Judgment)

Thus all shall acclaim sovereignty to God
Unto God who orders judgment
Who searches hearts on the Day of Judgment
Who uncovers deep things in judgment
Who ordains righteousness on the Day of Judgment

Who utters knowledge in judgment
Who is perfect, and shows compassion on the Day of Judgment
Who remembers His covenant in judgment
Who has compassion upon His handiwork on the Day of Judgment
Who makes pure those that trust in Him in judgment
Who divines peoples thoughts on the Day of Judgment
Who restrains His indignation on the Day of Judgment
Who is clothed in charity on the Day of Judgment
Who pardons iniquity in judgment,
Who is revered in praises on the Day of Judgment
Who forgives the people chastened by Him in judgment
Who answers His suppliants on the Day of Judgment
Who shows His mercy in judgment
Who observes secret things on the Day of Judgment
Who is Master of all in judgment
Who has compassion on His people on the Day of Judgment
Who preserves them that love Him in judgment
Who sustains His blameless ones on the Day of Judgment.

Commentary

This *piyyut* has been ascribed to Rabbi Elazar haKallir (eighth century). It is an alphabetical acrostic, with each verse beginning with a letter of the Hebrew alphabet. The theme of this liturgical poem is repeated numerous times throughout—namely that Rosh Hashanah is a Day of Judgment. The repeated refrain *"yom din"* (day of judgment) creates a mood of solemnity. The author lists the qualities of judgment associated with God the Judge, including God's attributes of mercy, compassion, and love. These attributes assure the truly repentant that God will forgive his or her sins. Interestingly the Jewish zodiacal sign for the month of Tishri, upon which Rosh Hashanah and Yom Kippur falls, is scales of judgment.

Uvechen Ten Pachdecha
(Let Your Awe Be Manifest)

And therefore, O Lord our God, let Your awe be manifest in all Your works, and a reverence for You fill all that You have created, so that all Your creatures may know You, and all people bow down to acknowledge You. May all Your children unite to do Your will with a complete heart. For we know, O Lord our God, that dominion is Yours, that Your might and power are supreme, and that Your name is revered over all You have created.

And therefore, O Lord, grant glory to Your people who serve You, praise to those who revere You, hope to those who seek You, and confidence to those who yearn for You. Bring joy to Your land, gladness to Your city, renewed strength to the seed of David, and a constant light to Your servants in Zion. May this come to pass quickly in our days.

And therefore, the righteous shall see and be glad, the just exult, and the pious rejoice in song, while transgression shall close its mouth and all wickedness shall disappear like smoke, when You remove the dominion of tyranny from the earth.

Commentary

Each of the paragraphs of this prayer begin with the Hebrew word *uvachen*—and therefore, reaffirming loyalty to a universal outlook and world unity, the well-being of Israel and the triumph of moral law. These paragraphs are included in each *Amidah* of the High Holy Days, and are ascribed to Rabbi Yochanan ben Nuri, who lived during the Hadrianic persecutions. The tyrannical power of the Romans likely gave rise to this prayer, which envisions a time when all people will unite in one fellowship to do God's will. Fear of God will thus be a restraint to man's inhumanity to man.

The second *uvachen* paragraph envisions an Israel that will be happy and joyous because of the renewed strength brought to it by God.

The final and third *uvachen* paragraph of this prayer is a vision of the future when the righteous will be glad and all the wicked will disappear forever.

Torah Reading for First Day of Rosh Hashanah

The biblical reading for the first day of Rosh Hashanah (Genesis, Chapter 21); tells of the birth of Isaac to Abraham and Sarah in their old age. Alarmed over Ishmael's disturbing influence upon Isaac, Sarah insists on the banishment of Hagar and her son Ishmael. Abraham appears perplexed, but receives divine assurance that it is all for the best, for it will be through Isaac that Abraham's name will be carried on. Hagar and Ishmael are miraculously saved from starvation and Ishmael becomes a man of war. The Torah reading concludes with the incident of a quarrel between the shepherds of Abraham and their neighbors. Desiring to put an end to ill will and controversy, Abraham makes a covenant of peace with Avimelech at Beer Sheba. Abraham planted a tamarisk tree at the place and offered worship to God.

The biblical reading's opening verse states that "God remembered Sarah." The theme of remembrance is one of the major ones during the Rosh Hashanah Additional Musaf Service. Rosh Hashanah commemorates the birthday of the world and the rebirth of humanity. According to a rabbinic tradition (*Rosh Hashanah*, 10b), Sarah gave birth to Isaac on Rosh Hashanah.

The *maftir* additional Torah reading for the first day of Rosh Hashanah is taken from the Book of Numbers 29:1–6, which describes the biblical description of Rosh Hashanah and the special sacrifices that were brought on this day: "And in the seventh month, on the first day of the month, you shall have a holy convocation. You shall do no manner of servile work. It is a day of blowing the horn unto you. You shall prepare a burnt offering for a sweet savor unto God: one young bullock, one ram, seven male lambs of the first year, without blemish . . . .

Haftarah for the First Day of
Rosh Hashanah

The reading from the Prophets (I Samuel 1:2–20), like the Torah reading, deals with the birth of a child. The Haftarah depicts Hannah giving birth to Samuel, whose life is consecrated to the service of God. Like Sarah, Hannah manifests serious concern for the spiritual welfare of her child. Her example teaches the importance of Jewish motherhood and raising a Jewish child: "And Hannah brought her child to the house of God while the child was young." (I Samuel 1:24)

Particularly noteworthy is the reference made in the Haftarah to a custom of annual family pilgrimages to Shiloh where the Ark of the Covenant was housed prior to David's selection of Jerusalem as the sight of the Temple.

Torah Reading for the Second Day of
Rosh Hashanah

The Torah reading for the second day of Rosh Hashanah is the twenty-second chapter of the Book of Genesis. The story in Hebrew is known as the *Akedah* (binding), because it deals with the attempted binding and sacrifice of Isaac by his father Abraham, whose faith was put to the supreme test when he was commanded to present his beloved son as a burnt offering on one of the mountains in the land of Moriah. According to rabbinic tradition, this was the tenth and the greatest of the trials that Abraham had to face, to prove that he was worthy of being the founder of the Jewish people.

This narrative also portrays the faith and obedience of the second Jewish patriarch, Isaac. Both his willingness and that of his father Abraham are symbolic of supreme trust and devotion as well as Jewish martyrdom followed by divine mercy. The story of the *Akedah* is also frequently recalled in the liturgy of the prayerbook.

The sounding of the ram's horn on Rosh Hashanah serves as a reminder of the horn of the ram that was sacrificed by Abraham in place of Isaac.

Haftarah for the Second Day of Rosh Hashanah

The prophetic portion for Rosh Hashanah's second day is a fine example of the hopefulness that faith in God engenders in people. Jeremiah the Prophet, who beheld the destruction of the First Temple in Jerusalem and the exile of the Israelites to Babylon, heartens the despairing Jews with a glowing picture of the restoration. He beautifully portrays the matriarch Rachel weeping disconsolately for her homeless children. God, however, comforts her with the assurance that here children will return to Zion after sincere and complete repentance. Ephraim, as the northern kingdom of Israel is called, is pictured as the prodigal child whom God loves with great compassion, and whom God takes to His heart when Ephraim expresses sincere remorse for his misdeeds. According to Jewish legend, when the Jewish exiles passed by the grave of Rachel she cried so bitterly that God Himself was moved by her tears, and said: "For your sake, O Rachel, I will lead the children of Israel back to their land."

Hineni (Behold)

In deep humility I stand and plead before you, God on high,
Great God who is enthroned above all praise
Hearken and give heed to my prayer.
Though my sacred task is unworthy
Though imperfect, and filled with awe,
I bow before Your holy presence
To crave compassion for my erring people.
O God of Israel's patriarchs
Their children's children send me as their voice
To pray for Your pardon and mercy,
To ask Your grace and Your continued love
Though I am unworthy of my mission, O God,
Though I do not stand without flaw in Your sight,
Do not condemn my people for my faults,
Consider their virtues, Righteous Judge
Forgive our transgressions,
And turn our affliction into joy.
You, great and mighty God, who listens to prayer,
Hear ours, and bless us all with life and peace.

Commentary

It is conjectured that *Hineni* was composed by a humble cantor
in the Middle Ages. In this supplication, the author is aware of his
immense responsibility in leading the congregation in worship. The
Talmud (*Rosh Hashanah* 34b) declares that, while on other occasions only the unlettered among the congregation fulfil their obligation by listening to the cantor's repetition of the *Amidah*, in the
case of the Musaf Additional Service even the most learned do so,
for very few are familiar with the new additions and insertions. In
this personal prayer he pleads to God that his rendering of the

prayers will be acceptable and unblemished. The Hineni prayer is chanted both on Rosh Hashanah and Yom Kippur immediately prior to the Musaf Additional Service.

Unetanneh Tokef (We Will Observe)

We will observe the great holiness of this day, for it is one of awe and trepidation. Thereon is Your dominion exalted. On this day we conceive You established on Your throne of kindness, sitting thereon in truth. We behold You, as Judge and Witness, recording all of our secret thoughts and acts and setting the seal thereon. You record all; You remember things that are forgotten. You unfold the records, and the deeds therein inscribed tell their own story, for the seal of every person's hand is set thereto.

The great shofar is sounded, and a still small voice is heard. The angels in heaven are dismayed and are seized with fear and trembling, as they proclaim: "Behold the Day of Judgment." The heavenly hosts are to be arraigned in judgment for in Your eyes even they are not free from guilt. All who enter the world do You cause to pass before You, one by one, as a flock of sheep. As a shepherd gathers his sheep and causes them to pass beneath his staff, so do You pass and record, count and visit, every living soul, appointing the measure of every creature's life and decreeing its destiny.

On New Year's Day the decree is written and on the Day of Atonement it is sealed, how many shall die and how many shall be born; who shall live and who shall die; who shall attain the measure of man's days and who shall not attain it; who shall perish by fire and who by water; who by sword and who by beast; who by hunger and who by thirst; who by earthquake and who by plague; who by strangling and who by stoning; who shall have rest and who shall go wandering; who will be tranquil and who shall be disturbed; who shall be at ease and who shall be afflicted; who shall become poor and who shall grow rich; who shall be brought low and who shall be exalted.

But repentance, prayer, and charity avert the severity of the decree.

Commentary

This prayer poem, figuring prominently in the Musaf Additional Service, is traditionally attributed to Rabbi Amnon of Mayence, a legendary martyr at the time of the Crusades (twelfth century). According to some, it was published by Rabbi Kalonymus ben Meshullam, an eleventh-century German liturgist.

This stirring poem, describing in exalted language the heavenly procedure on the day of judgment, has been the subject of a popular story, the oldest mention of which is found in the thirteenth-century work *Or Zarua* by Rabbi Isaac of Vienna. The story reads:

Rabbi Amnon, a wealthy scholar, was repeatedly but fruitlessly pressed by the Archbishop of Mayence to change his faith. On one occasion he went so far as to ask evasively for a three-day respite to consider. Upon reaching home, he would neither eat nor drink. He was sad at heart and wept bitterly because he had given the impression that he might renounce his belief in the unity of God. When he failed to appear at the end of three days, he was arrested and compelled to plead guilty. As a punishment, his hands and feet were cut off. On New Year's Day, Rabbi Amnon was brought to the synagogue at his own request. When the cantor was about to lead the congregation in the recitation of the *Kedushah,* Rabbi Amnon asked him to pause. Dying from his wounds, Rabbi Amnon recited the prayer *Unetaneh Tokef* and immediately died. Three days later he appeared to Rabbi Kalonymus ben Meshuallam in a dream and taught him this prayer that it might be introduced to all congregations.

The prayer depicts Rosh Hashanah and You Kippur as the days of heavenly judgment, when it is decreed "how many shall pass away and how many shall be born, who shall live and who shall die." ... But repentance, prayer, and charity avert the severity of the decree. The *Unetaneh Tokef* also mentions God's consideration of human weakness and His benevolence.

Vechol Maamineem (All Believe)

God holds in His hand the measure of judgment
And all believe that God is the faithful God.

God tries and searches into the most hidden secrets
And all believe that God knows the innermost thoughts.

God redeems from death and delivers from the grave
And all believe that God is the mighty Redeemer.

God alone is the Judge of all who come into the world;
And all believe that God is the true Judge.

God is called "I am that I am";
And all believe that God is, was, and will always be.

God's name is unchangeable and thus is God's praise;
And all believe that there is none besides God.

God remembers for their good those who are mindful of Him
And all believe that God remembers the covenant.

God apportions life unto all His creatures;
And all believe that God lives and endures.

God is good and beneficent to the wicked as well as to the good;
And all believe that God is good to all.

God knows the nature of all creatures;
And all believe that God fashions them all.

God is all powerful and all perfect
And all believe that God is omnipotent.

The Almighty dwells everywhere, even in the secret place;
And all believe that God alone is One.

God causes kings to reign, while all dominion is His
And all believe that God is the eternal Sovereign.

God guides every generation with His lovingkindness
And all believe that God keeps mercy.

God is patient and overlooks the evil of the rebellious
And all believe that God forgives.

God is exalted and guards those that revere Him
And all believe that God answers the silent prayer.

God opens His gate to them that call in repentance;
And all believe that God's hand is always open to receive them.

God waits for the wicked and delights when they return to
righteousness;
And all believe that God is just and righteous.

God is slow to anger and forbearing;
And all believe that God is difficult to arouse to anger.

God is merciful and God's compassion goes before His indignation;
And all believe that God is easy to reconcile.

God is just and before God the great and small are alike;
And all believe that God is the righteous Judge.

Commentary

This ninth-century twofold alphabetical acrostic has been traditionally ascribed to Yochanan ha-Cohen. Other historians have ascribed its authorship to Yannai of the seventh century. In its declaration that God holds in His hand the scales of justice, this prayer presents a theology in which God's characteristics and attributes are listed. Among these attributes of God are: God redeems, God is the Judge, God is eternal, God is unique, God is omnipotent, God is omnipresent, God is patient, and God is merciful.

Ochila L'El (I Hope in God)

I will hope in God; God's presence I will entreat; I will ask God for the gift of speech that in the congregation of the people I may sing of God's power and render joyful melody concerning God's deeds. The preparation of the heart is the concern of man, but the gift of speech comes from God. O God, open my lips that my mouth shall declare Your praise. May the words of my mouth and the thoughts of my heart be acceptable to You, O God, my Rock and my Redeemer.

Commentary

This prayer, of unknown authorship, is recited by the cantor as a personal prayer, in which the cantor seeks God's help. Realizing the importance of properly chanting the prayers for the congregation, the cantor in this prayer requests that his speech be worthy of God's praise.

Alenu (It Is Our Responsibility)

Let us adore the God of all, who formed the world from of old, that God has not made us like the heathens of the earth, nor fashioned us like the godless of the land. God has not made our destiny as theirs, nor cast our lot with their multitude. We bend the knee, bow in worship, and give thanks to the Sovereign of Sovereigns, the Holy Blessed One.

God stretches forth the heavens and laid the foundations of the earth. God's glory is revealed in the heavens above, and God's might is manifest in the loftiest heights. He is our God, and there is no other. In truth God is our Sovereign, there is none besides Him. Thus it is written in God's Torah: "Know that day and consider it in your heart that God is the God in the heavens above and on the earth below, and there is none else."

Commentary

The *Alenu* prayer, proclaiming God as Sovereign over a united humanity, has been recited as the closing prayer of the three daily services ever since the thirteenth century. According to an old tradition, Joshua, successor of Moses, composed it at the time he entered the Promised Land. It is generally held, however, that it was first introduced by Rav, founder of the Sura Academy in the third century of the common era, as an introduction to *Malchuyot*, the Sovereignty verses recited as part of the Musaf Additional Service of Rosh Hashanah.

The *Alenu* voices the vision of the future when all people will abandon idolatrous beliefs and when the world will be perfected by the universal recognition of God's sovereignty.

Malchuyot Sovereignty Verses

God shall reign for ever and ever. (Exodus 15:18)

God has beheld no iniquity in Jacob, neither has God seen perverseness in Israel. The Lord their God is with them and they raise their voices to honor their king. (Numbers 23:21)

God became King in Jeshurun when the heads of the people were gathered with all the tribes of Israel. (Deuteronomy 33:5)

For the sovereignty is God's, and God is the Ruler over the nations. (Psalm 22:29)

God reigns, God is robed with majesty; God is robed and girt with power; the world is set firm that it cannot be moved. (Psalm 93:1)

Lift up your heads, O you gates, and be lifted up, you everlasting doors that the Sovereign of glory may enter. "Who is the Sovereign of glory?" "The Lord of hosts, God is the King of glory." (Psalm 24:7–10)

Thus says the Lord of hosts, the Lord, Sovereign and Redeemer of Israel: "I am the first and I am the last, and besides Me there is no God." (Isaiah 44:6)

And redeemers shall ascend Mount Zion to judge Mount Esau and the sovereignty shall be God's. (Obadiah 1:21)

And God shall be Sovereign over all the earth; on that day God shall be One and God's name One. (Zechariah 14:9)

Hear O Israel, the Lord our God, the Lord is One. (Deuteronomy 6:5)

Commentary

The Musaf Additional Service for Rosh Hashanah includes the three central sections named *malchuyot* (verses of sovereignty), *zichronot* (remembrance verses), and *shofarot* (trumpet verses). The Mishnah (*Rosh Hashanah* 4:6), compiled in the second century of the common era, already mentions these three divisions as part of the ritual of the day. It also refers to the practice, still observed, of sounding the shofar between each of these three sections, and the provision that each of these three sections contain not less than ten verses from the threefold division of the Bible—three from the Five Books of Moses, three from the Prophets, and three from the Book of the Writings. Each of these collections is preceded by an introduction ascribed to the Babylonian teacher Rav of the third century of the common era.

The *malchuyot* verses all deal with the theme of God as King. God is Sovereign, and the salvation of people depends upon their acceptance of God as King.

Zichronot Remembrance Verses

And God remembered Noah and every living creature, and all the cattle that were with him in the ark; and God caused a wind to blow over the earth and the waters abated. (Genesis 8:1)

And God heard their groaning, and remembered His covenant with Abraham, Isaac, and Jacob. (Exodus 2:24)

Then will I remember my covenant with the patriarchs and I will remember the land. (Leviticus 26:42)

God has made a memorial for His wondrous works; God is gracious and full of compassion. (Psalm 91:4)

God has given food to them that revere Him. God will ever be mindful of His covenant. (Psalm 91:5)

And God remembered for their sake His covenant; God relented of His wrath according to the greatness of His mercies. (Psalm 106:45)

Go and proclaim so that Jerusalem may hear: Thus says God,

"I remember for you the devotion of your youth, the love of your espousals; how you chased after Me in the wilderness, in a land unsown." (Jeremiah 2:2)

Nevertheless I will remember My covenant with you in the days of your youth. And I will establish unto you an eternal covenant. (Ezekiel 16:60)

Is not Ephraim My beloved son, My beloved child, for even when I speak against him, I remember him with affection. Therefore, my heart yearns for him; yea, I will surely have compassion on him, says God. (Jeremiah 31:20)

For their sakes I will remember the covenant of their ancestors whom I brought forth out of the land of Egypt in the sight of the nations, to be their God. I am the Lord. (Leviticus 26:45)

Commentary

By reciting the *zichronot* verses of remembrance, the worshiper is heartened with the knowledge that God has never forgotten His people. God remembers the covenant that He made with the patriarchs concerning the future of the land and the people of Israel. To believe that God remembers and will continue to remember His people throughout history serves as a great source of comfort for the present and confidence for the future.

Shofarot Trumpet Verses

And it was on the third day, in the morning, there was thunder and lightning and a dense cloud over the mountain; there was a loud shofar blast and all the people in the camp trembled. (Exodus 19:16)

The sound of the shofar waxed louder and louder; Moses spoke and God answered him. (Exodus 19:19)

And all the people perceived the thunders and the lightnings and the voice of the shofar, and the mountain smoking; and when the people saw it, they trembled and stood afar off. (Exodus 20:15)

God manifested Himself with the sound of the shofar, the Lord amidst the sound of the shofar. (Psalm 47:6)

With trumpets and sound of the shofar, raise joyful voices before the Sovereign, the Lord. (Psalm 98:6)

Sound the shofar on the new moon and on the full moon for our festive day. It is a statute for Israel, and ordinance of the God of Jacob. (Psalm 81:4–5)

Praise God, halleluyah; praise God in His sanctuary; praise God in the mighty firmament. Praise God for His saving deeds. Praise God according to His abundant greatness. Praise God with the blast of the shofar; praise God with psaltery and harp. Praise God with timbrel and dance; praise God with stringed instruments and reed. Praise God with resounding cymbals; praise God with clanging cymbals. Let everything that has breath praise God. Halleluyah. (Psalm 150)

All you inhabitants of the world and dwellers on earth; when a banner is lifted up on the mountain, see you, and when the shofar is sounded, hear. (Isaiah 18:3)

On that day a great shofar shall be sounded; and they shall come who were lost in the land of Assyria, and they who were cast away in the land of Egypt; and they shall bow down to God on the holy mountain at Jerusalem. God shall be revealed to them, and God's arrows go forth as lightning. God shall sound the shofar, and shall go in the whirlwinds of the south. The Lord of hosts will defend them. (Zechariah 9:14)

On the day of your gladness, and on your festivals, and on new moons, you shall sound the shofar over your offerings; and they shall be a memorial before your God; I am the Lord your God. (Numbers 10:10)

Commentary

God revealed Himself on Mount Sinai to our ancestors amid the sounds of the shofar. The great shofar will ultimately herald God's redemption of Israel and all people. In the three shofarot verses from the prophetic books, the shofar sounds are identified with the messianic restoration of Israel. Amidst crowds worshiping in a rebuilt Temple in Jerusalem, the redeemed people of Israel will again sound the ram's horn on all of their holy days and festivals.

Hayom Te'amtzaynu (Today Save Us)

This day may You strengthen us. Amen.
This day may You bless us. Amen.
This day may You exalt us. Amen.
This day may You consider us for well being. Amen.
This day may You inscribe us for a happy life. Amen.
This day may You hear our supplication. Amen.
This day may You accept our prayer in mercy and favor. Amen.
This day may You uphold us with the power of Your righteousness. Amen.

Commentary

This prayer petitions God for His blessings of a happy life and well-being. The key Hebrew word is *hayom*—today, emphasizing that every day is a gift of life from God, if we only use it wisely.

YOM KIPPUR EVENING PRAYERS

Kol Nidrei (All Our Vows)

By the authority of the heavenly tribunal, and of the court below, with divine sanction and with the sanction of the holy congregation, we declare it lawful to pray together with those who have transgressed.

All vows, bonds, promises, obligations, and oaths wherewith we have vowed, sworn, and bound ourselves from this Day of Atonement to the next Day of Atonement, may it come to us for good. Of all these, we repent us in them. They shall be absolved, released, annulled, made void, and of none effect. They shall not be binding nor shall they have any power. Our vows shall not be vows, our bonds shall not be bonds, and our oaths shall not be oaths.

Commentary

The Aramaic formula for the dispensation of vows, recited on the eve of Yom Kippur, is more than a thousand years old. *Kol Nidrei* (all our vows) refers to vows assumed by an individual for himself alone, where no other persons or their interests are involved. The law in the Bible regarding vows is stated in this way: "When you make any vow to God, you must pay it without delay.... If you refrain from making a vow, you will not be held guilty. But you must be careful to keep any promise you have made with your lips." (Deuteronomy 23:22–24) Since a person runs the risk of either breaking or delaying to fulfill the vow made, Judaism advises to refrain from rash vows even if they are motivated by pious devotion.

On account of its great solemnity, Yom Kippur was chosen for the chanting of *Kol Nidrei*, which acquired intense significance during the period of persecutions in Spain. Many Jews in Spain and Portugal who had been forced to resign their faith in order to adopt a new religion attended the synagogue in secret at the risk of their lives and used *Kol Nidrei* as a form of renouncing the vows imposed upon them by the Inquisition.

The custom has been to recite *Kol Nidrei* three times, the first softly, like one who hesitates to enter the king's palace; the second somewhat louder; and the third even louder, like one who is accustomed to being a member of the king's court. The three chantings also provide additional time for latecomers to worship services to hear the Kol Nidrei. *Kol Nidrei* is chanted before sunset because dispensation of vows may not be granted on Sabbaths or holy days.

Ya'aleh (May They Rise)

May our supplications rise at nightfall
Our prayers approach Your presence from the dawn,
And let our exultation come at dusk.
May our voices rise in prayer at nightfall
Our righteousness ascend to You from dawn
And let redemption come to us at dusk.
O may our sorrows rise to You at nightfall
Our pardon issue forth from break of dawn,
And let our cries be heard by You at dusk.
May our liberation rise at nightfall
Our cleansing from all guilt come from the dawn,
And let Your grace be manifest at dusk.

May our merits rise to You at nightfall,
Our congregation plead with You from dawn,
And let Your glory shine for us at dusk.
May we know upon Your gates at nightfall,
Our joy and gladness come to us from dawn
And let our plea be granted us at dusk.
May our cries rise up to You at nightfall,
Our anguish reach Your presence from the dawn,
And turn to us in mercy, God, at dusk.

Commentary

The theme of this poem, *Yaaleh* (rise up), the author of which
is unknown, was suggested by the service of the Day of Atonement, which begins with *Kol Nidrei* in the evening, is resumed at
early dawn, continues through the day, and culminates at dusk.
The literary structural form of the poem is a reversed Hebrew
alphabetical acrostic, where each verse begins with a letter of the
Hebrew alphabet, beginning with the last letter, *tav.* In this prayer,
the author makes an emotional plea that the prayers of Israel ascend to heaven at nightfall and arrive before God's throne in the
early morning, so that salvation and redemption may come with
the dusk.

Ki Hinay Kachomer (As Clay)

As clay we are, as soft and yielding clay
That lies between the fingers of the potter.
At his will he moulds it thick or thin,
And forms its shape according to his fancy.
So are we in Your hand, God of love.
Your covenant recall and show Your mercy.

As stone are we, inert, resistless stone
That lies within the fingers of the mason
At his will he keeps it firm and whole
Or at his pleasure hews it into fragments.
So are we in Your hand, God of life.
Your covenant recall and show Your mercy.

As iron are we, as cold and rigid iron
That lies within the fingers of the craftsman.
At his will he forges it to shape
Or draws it boldy forth to lie unbended.
So are we in Your hand, God who saves.
Your covenant recall and show Your mercy.

As glass are we, as thick transparent glass
That lies within the fingers of the blower.
At his will, he blows it crystal clear,
Or melts it down to suit his whim or notion.
So are we in Your hand, gracious God.
Your covenant recall and show Your mercy.

As cloth are we, as formless, graceless cloth,
That lies within the fingers of the drape
At his will he shapes its lines and folds,
Or leaves it unadorned to hang unseemly.
So are we in Your hand, righteous God.
Your covenant recall and show Your mercy.

As silver are we, with metal dross alloyed
That lies within the fingers of the smelter,
At his will he fuses or refines,
Retains the slag or keeps it pure and precious,
So are we in Your hand, healing God.
Your covenant recall and show Your mercy.

Commentary

In this poem, a Hebrew alphabetical acrostic of unknown authorship, God is described as a craftsman shaping man's destiny. He is compared to the potter who molds the clay into various shapes, to the mason hewing the block of stone, to the smith bending the rigid steel, and so forth. The poem emphasizes man's dependence on his Maker and pleads for God's mercy.

Shema Kolenu (Hear Our Voice)

Heavenly father, heed our cry,
Give ear and grant our supplication.

Accept our words, our fervent prayer
Consider our meditation.

Rock divine, be with Your folk,
Cast not Your people from Your presence.

Without You, God, there is no hope,
Your life an aimless evanescence.

Lord, forsake us not, we pray,
Be our staff when our strength fails.

When youth to feeble age gives way,
Naught then but You, O God, avails.

You, O Father, was our hope
In all our days through joy and sorrow.

Be with us yet and to the end
Our Comforter in life's tomorrow.

Commentary

In *Shema Kolenu* the worshipper petitions God to have his or her words and prayers accepted so that he or she may be forgiven and reinstated in God's good favor.

Ki Anu Amecha
(We Are Your People)

We are Your people, and You are our God;
We are Your children, and You are our Father
We are Your servants, and You are our Master
We are Your congregation, and You are our portion.
We are Your inheritance and You are our lot,
We are Your flock, and You our shepherd,
We are Your vineyard and You our keeper,
We are Your work, and You our Creator.
We are Your faithful, and You our Beloved.
We are Your loyal ones, and You our Lord.
We are Your subjects, and You our Sovereign.
We are Your devoted people, and You are our exalted God.

Commentary

This prayer contains a series of expressions of affection and fondness between Israel and God whose sources are various parts of the Bible. They all express the covenantal relationship between God and the people, who are intimately bound one to another in a mutually exclusive agreement. The prayer reaches its climactic crescendo in its last verse, which states that "we are devoted to you and You are our exalted God."

Al Chet Confessional

For the sin which we have committed before You under compulsion or of our own free will.

For the sin which we have committed before You by hardening our hearts;

For the sin which we have committed before You unknowingly,

For the sin which we have committed before You with utterance of the lips;

For the sin which we have committed before You by unchastity,

For the sin which we have committed before You openly or secretly;

For the sin which we have committed before You knowingly and deceitfully,

For the sin which we have committed before You in speech;

For the sin which we have committed before You by wronging our neighbor,

And for the sin which we have committed before You by sinful meditation of the heart;

For the sin which we have committed before You by associating with impurity,

For the sin which we have committed before You by confession of the lips;

For the sin which we have committed before You by spurning parents and teachers,

For the sin which we have committed before You in presumption or in error;

For the sin which we have committed before You by violence.

For the sin which we have committed before You by profanation of Your name;

For the sin which we have committed before You by impure speech for the sin which we have committed before You by evil inclination.

For the sin which we have committed before You wittingly or unwittingly,

For all these, O God of forgiveness, forgive us, pardon us, and grant us atonement.

For the sin which we have committed before You by denying and lying,
For the sin which we have committed before You by bribery;
For the sin which we have committed before You by scoffing,
For the sin which we have committed before You in commerce,
For the sin which we have committed before You by demanding usurious interest,
For the sin which we have committed before You by stretching forth the neck in pride,
For the sin which we have committed before You by idle gossip,
For the sin which we have committed before You with wanton looks;
For the sin which we have committed before You with haughty eyes;
For the sin which we have committed before You by impudence;
For all these, O God of forgiveness, forgive us, pardon us, and grant us atonement.

For the sin which we have committed before You by casting off the yoke of Your commandments,
For the sin which we have committed before You by contentiousness;
For the sin which we have committed before You by ensnaring our neighbor,
For the sin which we have committed before You by envy;
For the sin which we have committed before You by levity,
For the sin which we have committed before You by being stiff-necked.
For the sin which we have committed before You by running to do evil,

For the sin which we have committed before You by talebearing;
For the sin which we have committed before You by vain oaths,
For the sin which we have committed before You by causeless hatred.
For the sin which we have committed before You by breach of trust,
For the sin which we have committed before You with confusion of mind.
For all these, O God of forgiveness, forgive us, pardon us, and grant us atonement.

Commentary

This confessional of one's sins is listed alphabetically with a double acrostic, each line beginning with the words "for the sin which we have committed." The prayer is repeatedly recited in the Yom Kippur service toward the end of each *Amidah*, to make the worshiper intensely aware of the need of a fuller mastery over his or her wandering impulses. The prayer is phrased in the plural because it is made collectively by the entire community, regarding itself responsible for many offenses that could have been prevented. A considerable number of sins mentioned in this prayer refer to offenses committed with the tongue, such as idle talk, slander, and talebearing. In the confession we are taught to examine ourselves in the spirit of humility and in the recognition that there is no person who is absolutely free from transgression.

YOM KIPPUR MORNING PRAYERS

Az Beyom Kippur (On Yom Kippur Day)

From time immemorial, You did on the Day of Atonement proclaim forgiveness, bringing light and pardon to Your people, forgiving the sins and transgressions of the congregation assembled in Your sanctuary with trust in You.

Sin grew stronger while my soul was asleep, but the Day of Atonement arouses me to knock at the gates of repentance pleading before the Creator of light and the Bestower of pardon.

May I behold Your light so that You may answer, "I have forgiven." O pass by our sins and do not condemn those who sin through ignorance.

We have done wickedly but You are just in all that has come upon us. We have sinned against You, O Sovereign of the Universe. Guide us with Your light that we may not suffer humiliation.

Good and forgiving God, righteousness is Yours; purify us in Your fountain, O You who are garbed in righteousness.

Day and night we pour out our hearts and souls in prayer. O let your light shine upon our distress.

Be merciful when You search our secret deeds and forgive us if we have strayed from You.

May we walk in the light of Your spirit and not depart from Your presence without Your grace.

Make the sins of Your people white as snow, for from You is the very source of life and kindness.

We pray to You who remembers the covenant, lead us in Your light as You did lead Elijah through the vale of darkness.

O God, who forgives the sheep of Your pasture, cover us with Your light as You did cover Moses when he beheld the rays of Your glory.

Answer us, O our Father, in our deep affliction. Rouse from sleep as with a shining light, Israel, lily of the valley.

Open for us the gates of prayer and admit our supplication. O You, who dwells on high, we seek Your presence.

Cleanse us of our impurity, so that transgression may leave no stain behind, and even as silver, seven times refined, may we be purified.

Draw us to Your salvation for the sake of Moses and Aaron, who proclaimed the holiness of the Day of Atonement.

Be our Shepherd as of yore and our life will be joyous. O God, hear us and do not delay.

We have poured out our stubborn hearts as water. Send forth the morning ray of pardon, O You who searches hearts.

Purify us and we shall be pure on this day of forgiveness. Listen, forgive us, and say: "I have forgiven."

Forgive on this holy day a people that aspires to holiness, O You who are mighty and holy.

Commentary

This poem, following the *Barchu* prayer, revolves around the theme of *or* (light). As a double Hebrew alphabetical acrostic, light alludes to the divine light within people when they come to confess before God and are forgiven. The poet recalls ancient times when during the Day of Atonement once a year, the High Priest would enter the Holy of Holies and pray on behalf of the people. Like our ancestors, we too seek the healing rays of inner light that result from a day of contrition.

Kadosh Adeer (The Holy Mighty One)

The Holy One is mighty in the heavens.
The Holy One has established His pardon on repentance.
The Holy One revealed His law to the people.
The Holy One rejoices when the sheep of His pasture are worthy of forgiveness.

The Holy One pardons the faithful.
The Holy One, all His people praise His mighty acts.
The Holy One remembers His people in love.
The Holy One delights in authentic repentance.
The Holy One pours His cleansing waters on those unclean.
The Holy One makes their sins as white as snow.
The Holy One seeks to forgive the transgression of Israel.
The Holy One appoints this day for atonement.
The Holy One pardons those who turn to Him in truth.
The Holy One revealed Himself on Mount Sinai.
The Holy One forgives those who in reverential awe obey Him.
The Holy One will graciously pardon iniquity.
The Holy One removes transgression.
The Holy One regards this day a fast for penitence.
The Holy One guides His faithful ones.
The Holy One is most kind and there is none besides Him.
The Holy One dwells in the high heavens.
The Holy One, angels proclaim His glory.

His sovereignty, I acknowledge amid the assembled throng. His glory is my faith; I seek God on this fast day to forgive my sins, to pardon my wrongdoing. May God answer me and say: "I have forgiven."

Commentary

This poem, a Hebrew alphabetical acrostic, is ascribed to Kalonymos of Lucca, father of Meshullam, a tenth-century poet. Throughout the poem it refers to God as *Kadosh* (Holy One). It is God who receives those who are penitent and who truly atone. God truly delights in one who repents with a full and complete heart.

Moreh Chata'im
(Guide for Transgressors)

You who show sinners the path in which to walk, teach the way to tread.

"I will extol You, my God, O King."

I will yoke dawn to night in continuous proclamation of Your sovereignty. You that abide to eternity, You are the peerless One.

"Every day will I worship You."

My heart yearns to worship You. I will stand watch to extol Your holiness.

"Great is God and greatly to be praised."

Fulfill the desire of them who hope for Your mercy, that Your faithful servants may rejoice.

"One generation shall laud Your works to another."

With supplication and fasting, they draw near to You; they were fashioned for Your honor, to serve You.

"The glorious splendor of Your majesty, they shall proclaim."

With reverence they tell of the splendor of Your kingdom, pledging unswerving loyalty to Your unity.

"They shall speak of the might of Your awe-inspiring acts."

This day a fourfold service they hold before You, and each day a sevenfold meditation of Your praise.

"They shall utter the fame of Your great goodness."

At morn I offer my supplication before You, and at evening You will blot out my transgressions.

"God is gracious and full of compassion."

God is our Rock and our delight. God will subdue our perversity that all may proclaim:

"God is good to all."

Raise up the city of Your joy; uplift her hallowed stones, precious as the jewels of a crown.

"All Your works shall give thanks to You, O God."
Your Levites and pious servants will harmoniously sing; priests in princely robes will serve You in righteousness.

"They shall speak of the glory of Your kingdom."
In its courts they shall flourish and thrive within its walls, bringing forth fruit in their old age.

"To make known to the sons of men God's mighty acts."
The pure and faithful will sing of Your glory when You have set Your throne within the everlasting House.

"Your kingdom is an everlasting kingdom."
When you gather the ransomed people to Your dwelling place, they shall invest You with might, like those of old that passed through the waves.

"God upholds all that fall."
Your people have gathered themselves in solemn assembly to declare Your goodness and offer their prayer.

"The eyes of all wait upon You."
May their confessions be as ancient offerings before You, and the utterance of Your witnesses be like sacrifices on Your altar.

"You open Your hand."
In Your mercy glance from the lattice of heaven, ready to forgive the people that call You blessed.

"God is righteous in all His ways."
O listen to the pleas of the people called by Your name, and be kind to those who observe Your festivals.

"God is near to all them that call upon Him."
You are my God who works wonders; may You accept our cry and disregard vile accusers.

"God will fulfill the desire of them that revere Him."
Grant hope to the person who casts his burden upon You; O Holy One, cover up our transgressions with Your love."

"God preserves all them that love Him."

O receive my prayer as if it were offered in the holy city of perfect beauty. Hear my voice and pardon my offense.

"My mouth shall speak the praise of God."

O Sovereign, who abides to eternity, reign alone in eternal supremacy, Most Holy God.

Commentary

This poem, written by Meshullam ben Kalonymous, is a double acrostic. The concluding line of the poem is an acrostic, spelling out the Hebrew name of the author, "Meshullam." The poem itself thanks God each day for the privilege one has of proclaiming God's sovereignty. The poet also pleads for the restoration of the Jerusalem Temple, where the Levites will again lead the Israelites in song and all Israel will assemble to offer a new song to God. Throughout the poem are interspersed verses from Psalm 145. (Ashray)

Imru Laylohim (Say You of God)

Say you of God, how great are Your works.

Say you of God: God is long suffering and of great power. God has established the mountains with strength. Wise of heart and mighty in strength, God gives strength to the tired.

Therefore be God exalted, for great is our God and all powerful.

Say you of God: God has built His lofty chambers in the heavens. From His heights He waters the hills. He has made a memorial of His wonders; by Him actions are weighed.

Therefore be God exalted who lays the beams of His chambers in the waters.

Say you of God: God is high and exalted above the summitless heavens. God covers Himself with light as with a garment. Might and greatness, strength and dominion are His.

Therefore be God exalted whose kingdom bears rule over all.

Say of you God: God is supreme over the myriads of holy beings and glorious in holiness. God's presence is in the sanctuary. All worship God in the beauty of holiness.

Therefore be God exalted, for He is my God and Sovereign. God's presence pervades the sanctuary.

Say you of God: His glory covers the heavens. God has spread forth the earth above the waters. When God's thunders roar in the heavens, there flows a tumult of waters.

Therefore be God exalted who stretches out the heavens as a curtain.

Say you of God: God has comprehended in a measure all the dust of the earth for his hand has founded the earth. His right hand has spanned the spacious skies; God has established them that they be not rent asunder.

Therefore be God exalted who dwells over the circle of the earth.

Say you of God: God is the life of the universe; by God's majestic name God has fashioned the universe; God has desired a sanctuary for all time, a place for God's eternal dwelling.

Therefore be God exalted who is known as the ancient of Days.

Say you of God: God is pure of sight; about Him is the gathering of waters, the thick clouds of the sky, the darkness of water. Many angels convey God's heavenly chariot beheld by the prophet in his vision.

Therefore be God exalted; the commandment of God is pure, enlightening the eyes.

Say you of God: God knows what is in the secret places of darkness; for darkness hides nothing from Him. God sets a limit to darkness, turning shadow and darkness to morning.

Therefore be God exalted who forms light and darkness.

Say you of God: God has established His throne in justice, the foundation of God's throne is righteousness and judgment. He is the God of justice and deals fairly with all.

Therefore be God exalted, yea, the Lord of hosts is exalted in judgment.

Say you of God: unto God alone sovereignty is ascribed. God lives forever with the contrite; God turns man to penitence, and says, "Return you with a humble spirit."

Therefore be God exalted, for sovereignty is God's.

Say you of God: God rules the universe by His might and all things are foreseen by Him and nothing is concealed. God's name is eternal and God's mercy is from everlasting to everlasting.

Therefore be God exalted. Blessed be the God of Israel from everlasting to everlasting.

Say you of God: God keeps mercy to a thousand generations, and from generation to generation God makes war against the forces of evil. God will sustain the righteous rulers; behold, light dwells with God in His habitation.

Therefore be God exalted whose memorial is from generation to generation.

Say you of God: God bears the heaven and the nethermost worlds. God listens to the needy and to the voice of supplication, yea God is attentive to the cry of prayer.

Therefore be God exalted, who is supreme, the God of gods, and the Lord of lords.

Say you of God: God is strong and powerful and brings to judgment those who rise against Him. God is the mighty warrior, combatting the forces of injustice.

Therefore be God exalted. God destroys wickedness and removes oppression.

Say you of God: God fashions the universe and in God's hands are all creatures, to make them great and give them strength. The eyes of all wait upon God who is all seeing.

Therefore be God exalted who is supreme over all.

Say you of God: God is righteous in all God's ways. God regards the upright and delights in the people who acclaim Him Sovereign. They who are blessed of God shall inherit the land.

Therefore be God exalted. Bless God, all His emissaries.

Say you of God: God calls the generations from the beginning. God determines the end from the beginning and has called a humble people to be in quest of His glory every day.

Therefore be God exalted who looks on the earth, and it trembles.

Say you of God: God's path is over the mighty water. God's heavens drop down showers. Behold, morning and evening we proclaim God's unity in the gate of God's courts.

Therefore be God exalted who is the Lord of hosts, enthroned above the cherubim.

Say you of God: The earth is full of God's praise. God sets aside the severe decree and turns away from destruction, accepting the cry of them that supplicate Him.

Therefore be God exalted. O God, how glorious is Your name in all the earth.

Commentary

This *piyyut,* composed by Meshullam ben Kalonymos, weaves many biblical verses together in its extolling of the awesome power of God. The concepts included in this poem include God's omnipotence, God as creator, God's righteousness, God's eternalness, and God's saving power. The refrain of each of the verses "say you of God" (in Hebrew, *imru layloheem*) is derived from Psalm 66:3: "Say you of God, how tremendous is Your work." An acrostic of the name of the author Meshullam is to be found in the lines of the last stanza of the poem.

Torah Reading for the Morning of
Yom Kippur

The Torah reading is taken from Leviticus, Chapter 16, and recalls the ancient sacrifices brought on the Day of Atonement. To impress the people with their communal responsibility for sin and the need for forgiveness, two goats were brought to the ancient Temple. Lots were cast to designate one goat for God, and the other for Azazel, symbol of wickedness. The first goat was offered in the prescribed manner as a burnt sacrifice. Upon the other goat, the High Priest placed his hand and confessed the sins of the people, after which the goat was sent away into the wilderness.

The ceremony graphically dramatized the casting away of the sins that the Israelites acquired in the wilderness, while the scapegoat became the symbol of wickedness, which was annually banished. When the Temple was destroyed this ceremony was discarded.

This reading was chosen because of its theme of atoning for sins and the need each year for cleansing oneself of transgression. After the reading of the passage from Leviticus 16, a second reading (that of the *maftir*), taken from Numbers 29:7–11, describes the additional communal sacrifices of the Day of Atonement.

Haftarah for the Morning of Yom Kippur

The prophetic portion for the morning of Yom Kippur is taken from the Book of Isaiah 57:14–58:14. In the Haftarah, the Prophet Isaiah chastises those who adhere to the form but violate the spirit of the Day of Atonement. Isaiah makes perfectly clear that the fasting in which God delights must result in a higher ethical standard: "Is not this the fast that I have chosen? To loose the fetters of wickedness, to undo the bands of the yoke ... to deal your bread to the hungry." (Isaiah 58:6–7) It is clear from these verses that fasting was intended to arouse sympathy for the plight of the hungry and the oppressed.

Yizkor Memorial Service

Following the chanting of the Haftarah on Yom Kippur is the *Yizkor* Memorial Service. During this service (which is also traditionally held on *Shemini Atzeret*, the last day of Passover and the second day of Shavuot), worshippers honor their dearly departed by reading prayers to their memory. According to the sixteenth-century codifier Rabbi Moses Isserles, the reason for the *Yizkor* prayers on Yom Kippur is that the departed are also in need of forgiveness. The central idea behind the *Yizkor* Memorial Service is that a person's life does not end with death of one's body, but that one's soul lives on. Additionally, the way in which one remembers his or her loved ones is by pledging charity and good deeds in their memory.

It is conjectured that the practice of reciting memorial prayers arose after the period of the first Crusade, when there was established the practice of reading the names of the martyred dead from the record books of the community. *Yizkor* prayers are generally recited only in congregations that follow the Ashkenazic rite, and not in those that follow the Sephardic rite.

Avodah Service (Temple Service)

The *Avodah* service comprises and describes the colorful service of the Kohen Gadol, the High Priest in the Temple on the Day of Atonement. It is based mainly upon the records preserved in the *Mishnah Yoma*, and was written by Rabbi Meshullam ben Kalonymous. During the service, the High Priest enters the Holy of Holies and makes confession for the sins of all of Israel.

The *Avodah* service ends with the prayer that the recollection of the ancient rites of Yom Kippur may serve to make the day effective for peoples as a day for creating true friendship with our fellow human beings and a day of full forgiveness of transgressions.

Eleh Ezkera (These Do I remember The Martyrology Service)

Following are some excerpts from the martyrology service:

These things I do remember and my heart is grieved. How the arrogant has devoured our people. In the reign of a certain emperor, ten sages, though innocent, were doomed to death by his command. The tyrant, searching our Torah for an excuse, yea, for a sword to slay us, found this law among our ordinances. "and he that steals a man and sells him, he shall surely be put to death." [Exodus 21:6]

Elated, he summoned ten great sages of our Torah and put to them this question: "What is the law if a man is found stealing his brother, one of the children of Israel, and makes merchandise of him and sells him?"

And the sages instantly replied, "That thief shall die...."

The cruel oppressor commanded that the ten sages be slain. Two of the great in Israel were first brought forth to the slaughter, the High Priest, Rabbi Ishmael, and Rabban Simeon ben Gamaliel, the Prince, ruler in Israel.

Then Rabban Simeon implored: "Slay me ere you slay him, lest I see the death of him who ministered to God."

The tyrant bade them to cast lots, and the lot fell on Rabban Simeon, who was immediately killed....

While he wept, the tyrant's daughter stood, and gazing upon the High Priest's handsome features, implored her father to spare his life, but her father refused to do so. They began to flay off the skin from Rabbi Ishmael's face....

Commentary

Following the *Avodah* service, recited during the Musaf Additional Service on Yom Kippur, an alphabetical poem bearing the title of *Eleh Ezkera* is read, describing the martyrdom of ten sages who died for the sanctification of God's name. The events referred to likely took place during the Hadrianic persecution following the year 135 of the common era. The fate meted out to the ten men of learning is graphically described in this prayer. Among the ten martyrs was the renowned Rabbi Akiva, who died with a smile on his lips in obedience to the verse: "And you shall love your God with all your life," which Akiba interpreted to mean: "Even if your life is demanded."

MINCHA AFTERNOON YOM KIPPUR SERVICE

Torah Reading

The scriptural reading for Yom Kippur afternoon is the eighteenth chapter of the Book of Leviticus, which condemns adultery and many other immoralities. Israel is warned to shun the licentious ways of the heathen Canaanites with whom they were to come into contact. It was likely selected to impress upon the Israelites the need of maintaining high standards of purity, chastity, and formal morality. It also reminds the worshipper of the importance of self-control, which has proven to be an important factor in the survival of the Jewish people.

The Haftarah: Book of Jonah

The prophetic reading selected for Yom Kippur afternoon is the entire Book of Jonah, the fifth book of the twelve Minor Prophets. The story of Jonah is well-known. Ordered by God to prophesy the destruction of Nineveh for its wickedness, Jonah attempted to escape from the divine command by sailing from the land of Israel. After his wonderful deliverance from drowning by being swallowed by a large fish, Jonah was obedient to a second commission from God. He went to Nineveh and there proclaimed that it would be destroyed in forty days. God spared the city when He saw the repentance of its people.

The Book of Jonah, containing the noblest expression of the universality of religion, is designed to show that kindness of heart and readiness to repent may be found everywhere among people.

The episode of the great fish swallowing Jonah has been interpreted figuratively as the captivity that swallowed up Israel. The deliverance from exile has been linked to being disgorged alive from the mouth of the devouring beast.

The Book of Jonah clearly shows that the compassion of God extends to all His creatures, even those who are as sinful as the people of Nineveh.

NEILA EVENING SERVICE

El Norah Aleelah (God That Does Wondrously)

God that does wondrously
God that does wondrously
Pardon at Your people's cry
As the closing hour draws near.

Few are Israel's sons, and weak,
You, in repentance, they seek,
O regard their anguished cry
As the closing hour draws near.

Souls gripe before You poured,
Agonize for deed and word;
"We have sinned: Forgive" they cry,
As the closing hour draws near.

Heal them. Let their trust in You
Turn aside wrath's dread decree
Doom them not, but heed their cry
As the closing hour draws near.

Mercy, grace for these bowed low
But upon the oppressor proud
Judgment for his victim's cry
As the closing hour draws near.

For our father's righteousness,
Save us now in our distress;
Make us happy with freedom's cry,
As the closing hour draws near.

Join O Shepherd, as of old,
Zion's with Samaria's fold;
Call Your flock with tenderest cry
As the closing hour draws near.

Elijah, Michael, Gabriel,
Come, the hoped-for tidings tell;
Let redemption be your cry
As the closing hour draws near.

God that does wondrously,
God that does wondrously,
Pardon at Your people's cry
As the closing hour draws near.

Commentary

This hymn is attributed to the Spanish Jewish poet Moses ibn Ezra and is used in the Sephardic ritual. Chanted at the beginning of *Neila*, it consists of eight stanzas whose theme is the mercy and grace of God. God listens to prayers, pardons transgressors, and will grant them another year of life and health.

Petach Lanu Shaar
(Open For Us the Gate)

Open the gates, the gates of the Temple
Swift to Your sins who Your truths have displayed.
Open the gates, the gates that are hidden,

Swift to Your sons who confess and seek grace.
Open the gates of the heavenly armies,
Swift to Your sons, Judah's tearful-eyed race.
Open the gates, the radiant portals,
Swift to Your sons who are lovely and pure.
Open the gates of the crown of fidelity,
Swift to Your sons who in God rest secure.

Commentary

This *piyyut* was written by Eleazar Kalir, and recalls the ancient rites during Temple times for the closing of the gates on Yom Kippur. The last service on Yom Kippur, *Neila* (closing), preserves the name of the final Temple ceremony when at the end of the day, before the closing of the gates, the priests dismissed the people.

As the gates of the heavens are about to be closed, the prayer asks that the gate be opened wide so that all may be cleansed of their sins and transgression.

Umee Ya'amode
(Who Could Live On)

Our God and God of our ancestors,
Who could stand if sin remained unshriven,
And who abide, did You his doom fulfill?
But it is Yours to say, "I have forgiven."
O guard Your attribute of mercy.

Abash us not, our poor estate beholding
Our longed-for knowledge of Your ways complete
Intelligence in young and old unfolding.
Make strong to follow You Your servant's feet.

Your shelter throw over penitent transgressors,
So shall they flourish and no longer pine;
The lost and exiled loose from their oppressors,
That they may freely offer at Your shrine.

Accept our words as ancient sacrifices,
When joined with righteousness, not merely breath;
Our pleader heed, destroy his enemy's device;
You love life and not the sinner's death.

Establish us within Your Face's shining,
Annul our sins and save us from the grave;
Before we call, our unsaid words divining
Accept the offerings of our mother we crave.

Your people's needs are large, their knowledge broken,
Their wants and wishes they can scarcely express;
Listen to their thought before it's spoken
Great God, so awesome in Your mightiness.

Bereft are we of all the holy masters,
In every form of prayer eloquent;
Hence grows the daily tale of our disasters,
And hence salvation tarries in descent.

We lack the heart for prayer's true relation,
For we have sinned, rebelled, and gone astray;
Mere alms the substance of our supplication,
When in Your house at night we stand and pray.

Vain-spun O God, the pleader's specious seeming,
Accept my plea as though a gift I brought;
And in Your crown, O set my prayer gleaming,
O God, whose girdle is of power wrought.

With pleasure hear my humble cry forgiving,
As though I were of goodness unalloyed;
Inscribe us all for life and happy living,
Suspender of the earth upon the void.

Stretch out Your hand and take my true contrition,
Beloved, pardon every evil deed;
And grant them good who at the dawn petition
O God, the shield and buckler of my need.

Commentary

This is a fusion of two liturgical poems by two different authors. The first half was composed by Solomon ben Judah ha-Bavli (tenth century), whose name, "Shelomo Hakatan," is the acrostic formed by the first letters of the last two stanzas. The second half of the poem beginning with the words *merubim tzarchei amecha* (your people's needs are large) is by Rabbi Joseph ben Isaac of Orleans, France (twelfth century). The full text is a complete Hebrew alphabetical acrostic concluding with an acrostic of the author's name, "Yosef bar Yitzchak."

In the first half of the poem, the main point is that God needs to forgive people, and cannot hold people fully accountable for their mistakes. In the poem's latter half, the poet says that while our needs are many, our ability to express ourselves is limited. Therefore, even though our prayers will always be inadequate, we pray that they will find favor in God's eyes.

Zechor Brit (Remember the Covenant)

Remember the covenant of Abraham, and the binding of Isaac. Turn back the captivity of the tents of Jacob, and save us for the sake of Your name.

You, mighty Redeemer, redeem us for Your own sake; Behold
how powerless we are, how few are our pious people, and there is
none to supplicate for us. O return in mercy toward the remnant
of Israel; Save us for the sake of Your name.
The holy city of Jerusalem and the provinces
Are become a reproach.
All their treasures are no more;
Nothing remains for us but the Torah
O turn back the captivity of the tents of Jacob
And save us for the sake of Your name.

Commentary

This prayer is part of a penitential psalm by Gershom bar Judah
(known as Meor Hagolah—"Light of the Exile"), born at Metz in
960. In the prayer we petition that God be mindful of His covenant with our ancestors so that we are saved and redeemed for
the sake of God's name.

Ezkerah Elohim (I Remember, God)

I remember, God, and I am deeply troubled,
When I see every city built on its own site
While Jerusalem, the city of God is razed to the ground;
Yet for all this, our faith in You does not falter.

O attribute of mercy, be moved compassionately toward us;
Supplicate your possessor, the Eternal,
And entreat for mercy for your people.
"For every heart is faint and every head is weary."

On the thirteen attributes of God, do I rely,
And on the flowing tears of contrite hearts;

Therefore have I poured out my prayer to Him who searches hearts.
In these do I have faith, and in the merit of the ancestors.

O You who hears weeping, hear us.
Pour out our tears in Your heavenly urn.
Deliver us and forgo Your dread decrees,
For unto You our eyes turn evermore.

Commentary

This *piyyut* was composed by Amitta ben Shephatiah in the late ninth century. The author, whose name, "Amittai," is the acrostic formed by the first four Hebrew letters of the four stanzas, lived in Italy. Greatly despondent, the author compares the razed city of Jerusalem with other people who had rebuilt their lands. Invoking God's thirteen attributes, the author is strengthened in his belief that God will treat His people Israel with great compassion and mercy, and their prayers will be heard and they will be saved.

Shema Yisrael (Hear O Israel), *Baruch Shem Kavod* (Blessed Be the name), and *Adonai Hu Eloheem* (The Lord, He Is God)

At the end of the *Neila* service, the fast of the Day of Atonement concludes with the recitation of: "*Shema Yisrael Adonai Eloheinu Adonai Echad*" (Hear O Israel, the Lord our God, the Lord is One) recited once, "*Baruch Shem Kavod Malchuto Le'olam Va'ed*" (Blessed be the Name of His glorious Kingdom forever and ever) said three times, and "*Adonai Hu Eloheem*" (The Lord, He is God) recited seven times.

The last phrase, The lord He is God, is associated with the incident in the eighteenth chapter of the First Book of Kings when Elijah helps to demonstrate God's power over the pagan god Baal.

In verse 19, the people, overwhelmed and awed by God's great power, fall on their faces and proclaim *"Adonai Hu Eloheem"*—The Lord, He is God. These words provide a powerful conclusion to the Yom Kippur worship service. This is followed by one long blast of the shofar—the *tekiah gedolah*—and the final wish *"leshanah haba'ah beyerushalayim"*—next year in Jerusalem!

FIFTEEN

THE DAYS OF AWE
IN JEWISH LEGEND

ROSH HASHANAH

Rosh Hashanah in modern parlance is often called the holiday of "the second chance." God allows people to repent for their mistakes, giving them an opportunity to improve upon their behavior and quality of their lives. Rosh Hashanah is thus a time for people to renew themselves and resolve to improve upon their past and strive to become better people.

References to Rosh Hashanah are found throughout the Talmud, with a special talmudic tractate called *Rosh Hashanah*. Other references to Rosh Hashanah, especially the legendary ones, are found in a variety of midrashic legendary texts. Following are examples of these texts.

1. Because of the great solemnity surrounding the festival of Rosh Hashanah, a whole month was ordained by the rabbis as a preparatory period. Also during this month, called Elul, the custom was to sound the shofar at each daily service, as a way of arousing the

people to begin to think seriously about repentance. The period concluded on Yom Kippur, and was later extended to the seventh day of Sukkot. A hint regarding the length of this period is found in the forty days that Moses, according to the biblical account, spent in heaven before receiving the second tablets. These forty days started on the first of Elul and ended on Yom Kippur. The following midrash illuminates this preparatory period.

It was taught: On the first of the month of Elul, the Holy One, blessed by the One, said to Moses: "Come up to Me to the mountain." (Deuteronomy 10:1) This was the time when Moses went up to receive the second tablets of the commandments. The sounds of the shofar were trumpeted throughout the encampment, which was the signal to the Israelites that Moses had ascended the mountain. Thus the people would not accidentally turn to idolatry.

The Holy One, blessed be He, was exalted through the sound of that shofar, as it is written, God ascends amid the *teruah*, God amidst the sound of the shofar. (Psalm 47:6)

Thus, the sages decreed that each year the shofar be blown from the beginning of the month of Elul through its entirety. This is to warn the people to repent, as it is written, "Can a shofar be blown in a city and the people not tremble?" (Amos 3:6), and also in order to confuse Satan. (*Pirkei d'Rabbi Eliezer* 46)

2. On the eve of Rosh Hashanah, traditional Jews customarily rise for penitential prayers two or three hours after midnight. Some stay up all night reciting these so-called *selichot* (prayers asking God for forgiveness), and thus this night has been called "the night of remembering the covenant." On this night Jews ask God to remember the covenant of their ancestors and to be shielded for their merit. The following story from the Talmud illustrates this custom.

When Israel sinned in the wilderness, Moses stood before the Holy One, blessed be He, and recited many prayers and supplications before Him, but was not listened to . But when Moses recited "remember Your servants Abraham, Isaac and Jacob, he was listened to immediately. (Talmud, *Shabbat* 30a)

2. As part of the preparations for the Day of Judgment, we also find the custom of fasting on the day before Rosh Hashanah. The basis for this unique custom can be found in the following legend:

It is written, "And you shall take for yourselves on the first day the fruit of beautiful trees, branches of palm trees, twigs of myrtle trees, and willows of the brook." (Leviticus 23:40)

Why does this verse refer to the "first day"? Does not the festival of Sukkot fall on the fifteenth of Tishri?

This refers to the first day of the new accounting of transgression.

Here is an analogy to this. One of the king's provinces owed taxes to the king but had not paid. The king gathered his army and set out to collect the overdue taxes. As the king approached within ten miles of the province the most prominent people came out to greet him.

They said, "We have nothing and cannot pay."

The king then cancelled one third of the debt.

As the king approached even closer to the province the middle level of people came out to great him and plead their cause.

The king then cancelled the entire debt.

The king in this analogy symbolizes the Holy One, Blessed be He. The inhabitants of the province are the Jewish people who sin all year and accumulate a large debt.

On the day before Rosh Hashanah, the most prominent among the Jews fast, and the Holy One, Blessed be He, forgives one third of their guilt. During the period of the Ten Days of Repentance, the middle level fasts, and the Holy One, Blessed be He, forgives another third of the guilt of the Jewish people. On Yom Kippur, everyone in the community fasts, and the Holy One, Blessed be He, forgives their entire guilt.

During the short amount of time between Yom Kippur and Sukkot people are preoccupied with the *mitzvah* of the sukkah and lulav. They do not have the opportunity to sin. Thus, the beginning of the festival of Sukkot is called "the first day" of the new accounting of transgression. (*Tanchuma Emor* 22)

3. In this next talmudic section, we learn that those who fast on the day before Rosh Hashanah are nevertheless expected to bathe, get a haircut, and dress in white garments.

Rabbi Simon said, "It is written, 'For what great nation is there that has deities close to it, as is our God whenever we call out to Him?' " (Deuteronomy 4:7)

Rabbi Chanina and Rabbi Joshua explained: "What other nation can compare to this nation in its familiarity with the laws and customs of its lords? In the way of the world, if a person is scheduled to go on trial he puts on black garments, wraps himself in a black cloak, lets his beard grow, and does not cut his fingernails, since he does not know what his verdict will be. This is not the custom of the Jewish people. They put on white garments and dress themselves in white cloaks, trimming their hair and fingernails. They eat and drink and are joyful on Rosh Hashanah. For they are very confident that God will perform a miracle for them. (Jerusalem Talmud, *Rosh Hashanah* 1:3)

4. The following talmudic teaching scrutinizes the historical background of Rosh Hashanah and all of the momentous events that occurred on this date. (i.e., the first of Tishri)

It was taught: Rabbi Eliezer says, "The world was created during the month of Tishri. Our forefathers were born during Tishri. Our forefathers died during Tishri. Our forefather Isaac was born on Passover. Sarah, Rachel, and Chanah conceived on Rosh Hashanah. Joseph was released from prison on Rosh Hashanah. Our ancestors were freed from their labors in Egypt on Rosh Hashanah, although they were not actually released from Egypt until the month of Nisan. And the ultimate redemption will come during the month of Tishri."

. . . It is also taught: Rabbi Eliezer says, "How do we know that the world was created during Tishri?"

It is written, "And God said, let the earth bring forth vegetation, plants yielding seed, and trees bearing fruit. . . . [Genesis 1:11] During which month does the earth bring forth vegetation and do the trees grow fruit? I would assume that it is Tishri. Also, that time was a time of rainfall and the rains came down and made the land blossom, as it is written, "and a mist arose from the land and watered the entire face of the earth." [Genesis 2:6], a further proof that the world was created during Tishri, the rainy season.

. . . . Rabbi Eliezer said, "How do we know that our forefathers were born during Tishri?"

It is written, "And all the Israelites gathered around King Solomon during the Month of the Mighty on the festival." [Kings I, 8:2] The reference to Tishri as "the Month of the Mighty" indicates that the Mighty Ancients were born during this month. . . .

How do we know that Sarah, Rachel, and Chanah were conceived on Rosh Hashanah?

Rabbi Elazar said: "This is derived from the parallel expressions of two different Hebrew words meaning 'remembering.'" It is written of Rachel, "And God remembered Rachel [Genesis 30:22], and it is written of Chanah, "And God remembered her [Samuel I 1:19].

We find the same Hebrew word used in reference to Rosh Hashanah in that which is written, "a remembrance of *teruah*." [Leviticus 23:24] Having established that Chanah conceived on Rosh Hashanah, we can now determine when Sarah conceived. The same Hebrew word is used in that which is written of Chanah, "for God remembered Chanah [Samuel I 2:21], and in that which is written about Sarah, "and God remembered Sarah." [Genesis 21:1] This indicates that Chanah and Sarah conceived at the same time of the year.

Joseph was released from prison on Rosh Hashanah. How do we know this?

It is written, "Blow the shofar on the new moon, for it is a law for Israel . . . as a testament to Joseph did he establish it when he went out to the land of Egypt. [Psalms 81:4–6]

Our ancestors were freed from their labors in Egypt on Rosh Hashanah. How do we know this?

It is derived from the parallel expression of the Hebrew word for burden in that which is written, "From under the burdens of Egypt [Exodus 6:6] and in that which is written of Joseph, "I removed his shoulder from the burden." [Psalms 81:17]

They were redeemed from Egypt during Nisan but the ultimate redemption will come during Tishri. This is derived from the mentioning of the shofar in reference to Rosh Hashanah in that which is written, "blow the shofar on the new moon" (Psalms 81:4) and in reference to the ultimate redemption in that which is written, "and it shall be on that day that a great shofar will be sounded." (Isaiah 27:13) (Talmud, *Rosh Hashanah* 10b)

5. Rosh Hashanah is also known a "Yom Hadin," the Day of Judgment. This legendary story explains the reason why.

It was once taught in the name of Rabbi Eliezer: The world was created on the twenty-fifth of Elul. The view of Rav is in agreement with the teaching of Rabbi Eliezer. For we have learned in the shofar blessing composed by Rav: "This day, on which was the beginning of work, is a memorial of the first day, for it is a statute for Israel, a decree of the God of Jacob. On it sentence is also pronounced upon countries, which of them is destined to the sword and which to peace, which to famine and which to plenty. Each separate creature is visited on that day and recorded for life or death."

Thus you are left to conclude that on New Year's Day, in the first hour the idea of creating man entered God's mind, in the second hour God consulted with the ministering angels, in the third hour God assembled Adam's dust, in the fourth God kneaded it, in the fifth God shaped him, in the sixth hour God made him into a lifeless body, in the seventh God breathed a soul into him, in the eighth God brought him into the Garden of Eden, in the ninth God warned him against eating of the fruit of the tree of knowledge, in the tenth he transgressed, in the eleventh he was judged, and in the twelfth hour he was pardoned. "This," said the Holy One, blessed be He, to Adam, "will be a sign to your children. As you stood in judgement before Me on this day and came out with a free pardon, so too will your children in the future stand in judgment before Me on this day and they too will come out from My presence with an unmerited pardon." When will this occur? In the seventh month, in the first day of the month [i.e., Rosh Hashanah] (Leviticus Rabbah 29:1)

6. This midrashic folktale comments on the theme of renewal and finding a new and improved way for the new year.

Once our master Rabbi Chayyim of Zans told this parable:
A man had been wandering in a forest for several days, and lost in the forest he could not find his way out. Suddenly he saw

another person approaching him and his heart became filled with joy.

"Now I will most assuredly find the right way out," he thought. When the two neared one another, he asked the man, "Brother, tell me, which is the right way. I have been wandering for several days and am lost."

The other answered, "Brother, I do not know the right way either. I too have been wandering for many days. But this much I can tell you. Do not take the way that I have been taking, for that will lead you astray. Come, let us look for a new way together."

Our master added, "So it is with us. One thing for sure, I can tell you. The way we have been following thus far is not the right way, for that way leads us further away from the right path. Let us look for a new way." (Rabbi Chayyim of Zans)

7. This talmudic comment relates the meaning of the four different New Years in the Jewish year:

There are four New Years. The first is on the first day of Nisan. This is the New Year for kings and festivals. The first of the month of Elul is the New Year for the tithe of cattle. The first of the month of Tishri is the New Year for the reckoning of the years, and for release and jubilee years for planting and the tithing of vegetables. The first of the month of Shevat is the New Year for trees, according to the School of Shammai, but the School of Hillel says it is on the fifteenth of Shevat.

At four seasons judgment is passed upon the world. At Passover, it occurs with respect to produce. At Shavuot, in respect of fruit. At the New Year all creatures pass before God like children at Maron, as it is written, God that fashions the heart of them all, that considers all of their doings. [Psalms 33:15] And on the festival of Sukkot, judgment is passed in respect of rain. (Talmud, *Rosh Hashanah* 1, 1–2)

8. In this selection God's ministering angels are told to defer to the human court in order to determine the exact day of the New Year.

Rabbi Pinchas and Rabbi Chilkiah taught in the name of Rabbi Simon: When all of the ministering angels gather before the Holy One and say, "Master of the Universe, what day is New Year's day?" God replies, "Why are you asking Me? Let us, both you and Me ask the court on earth."

Rabbi Hoshaiah taught, "When the earthly court decrees 'Today is the New Year,' the Holy One tells the ministering angels, 'Set up the judicial dais. Call the advocates to defend and to prosecute. For My children have announced that today is New Year's Day.' "

If, however, the court has decided to intercalate the year and move the New Year to the next day, the Holy One then tells the ministering angels, "Remove the judicial platform, dismiss all of the advocates, since My children have announced, 'Tomorrow is New Year's Day'..." (Jerusalem Talmud, 1:30)

9. The Hallel Psalms of Praise are recited on major Jewish festivals, expressing gratitude for God's dependability and redemptive qualities. Interestingly, Hallel is not recited on Rosh Hashanah nor on Yom Kippur. This selection explains the reason why.

Rabbi Abbahu taught: The ministering angels spoke up to the Holy One saying, "Master of the Universe, why do the Israelites not recite the psalms of praise before You on New Year's Day and on the Day of Atonement?"

God replied, "Is it possible that while the King is seated on His throne of judgment, with books of death open before Him, that the Israelites should be chanting hymns of praise?" (Talmud, *Rosh Hashanah* 32b)

10. In the High Holy Day liturgy we ask God numerous times to inscribe us in the Book of Life. This selection expands upon the High Holy Day metaphor of God and His Book of Life, obviously in an attempt to be certain that even the common person understands the principle of reward and punishment. In this talmudic passage, three different books are presented as possibilities.

Rabbi Kruspedai said in the name of Rabbi Yochanan: Three heavenly books are opened on the New Year. One is for the completely wicked person, one for the totally righteous person, and one for the intermediate. The righteous are inscribed definitively in the book of life, and the wicked are inscribed in the book of death. The doom of the intermediate is suspended from the New Year until the Day of Atonement. If they are deserving, they are inscribed in the book of life. If they do not fare well, they are then inscribed in the book of death.

Rabbi Abin asked, "What text tells us that this is so?" Let them be blotted out of the book of the living, and not be written with the righteous. "Let them be blotted out of the book" refers to the book of the wicked. "of life" refers to the book of the righteous. "And not be written with the righteous," this is the book of the intermediate. . . . (Talmud, *Rosh Hashanah* 16b)

11. God has been portrayed throughout Jewish history both as a God of stern judgment as well as a God of compassionate mercy. This selection attempts to explain God's merciful traits, based upon the theological concept of the "merit of our ancestors." This concept implies that the good deeds of our ancestors throughout the

ages will contribute to the welfare of our descendants. It has also been interpreted to imply that a person is best able to advance on the road to moral perfection if he or she starts with the accumulated spiritual heritage of righteous ancestors.

How did the Holy One, blessed be He, ordain the measure of mercy to accompany the measure of justice? Rabbi Chanina said, When the Holy One, blessed be He, was about to create the world, He saw the wicked deeds of the generation of Enosh, the generation of the deluge, the generation of the dispersion of the races of human beings, the acts of the people of Sodom. It was then that God no longer wished to create the world.

But then the Holy One, blessed be He, returned and observed all of the deeds of the righteous—of our ancestors Abraham, Isaac, and Jacob, and of all the other righteous. And when God returned and observed these, God said, "shall I not create the world because of the wicked? I will indeed proceed with the creation of the world, but as for those who sin, it will not be difficult to rebuke them."

However, when God was about to create the world using only the sole measure of His justice, God could not do so because of the meritorious deeds of the righteous, for who justice by itself would be too severe a decree. When God was about to create the world using only His measure of mercy, He could not bring Himself to do it, because of the horrible deeds of the wicked. What did God then decide to do? God brought the measure of justice and mercy into partnership, and created the world, as it written, "In the day that the Lord [of mercy and the] God [of justice] made heaven and earth." (Genesis 2:4)

Therefore David said: Master of the Universe, had You not judged Adam with mercy at the time that he ate of the forbidden tree, he would not have been sustained for even one single hour. And even as You judged him with mercy, so did You ordain, beginning with him, that this New Year's Day, You would judge his children with mercy. "Forever, O God, Your word stands fast." (Psalm 119:89) What is implied by 'stands fast?' Your word which You ordained for Adam still stands: even as You judged him with mercy, so You judge forever all the generations after him with mercy. Thus it says, "forever, O Lord." (*Peskita Rabbati* 40:2)

12. This midrashic text illustrates God's merciful judgment on the Gentile community in a most interesting way.

Rabbi Levi said, "God judges the Gentiles in mercy. How? God judges them at night when they are peaceful and do not sin. Why does God do this? Because God does not desire to punish even the wicked. For is there a potter who is desirous that his vessels be broken? But God judges Israel and righteous gentiles during the daytime when they perform good deeds." (*Peskita Rabbati* 41, 3)

13. There is a well-known legend that states that Sarah gave birth to Isaac on Rosh Hashanah. However, there is a lesser known statement that the very first human being, Adam, was created on Rosh Hashanah. On that very same day he sinned, repented, and was forgiven. Thus Rosh Hashanah was historically made into a most proper way for doing repentance.

It is written, "Forever, O God, are You established in the heavens" (Psalms 119:89), and it is also written, "Before Your judgment do they stand on this day" (Psalms 119:91), the inference being that this day had been established as a day of judgment from the very beginning of the creation of the world.

Rabbi Eliezer says, "The world was created on the twenty-fifth day of Elul."

This explanation is based on that which has been taught: During the Rosh Hashanah prayers we say, "This day marks the beginning of your deeds." This means the following: On Rosh Hashanah, Adam, the first man, was created. During the first hour of the day, God conceived the plan of creating a human being. During the second hour, God consulted the counsel of the angels. During the third hour, God collected the dust from which He would make the first human. During the fourth hour, God kneaded it, and during the fifth hour, He shaped it. During the sixth hour, God completed the form. During the seventh hour, God breathed a soul into it. During the eighth hour, God led the man into the Garden of Eden. During the ninth hour, the man was commanded not to eat from the Tree of Knowledge. During the tenth hour, he transgressed that command. During the eleventh hour, he was judged. During the twelfth hour, he was granted amnesty.

The Holy One said to Adam, "Just as you stood before Me today and were granted a pardon, so too, in the future, will your descendants stand before Me to be judged on this day and granted pardon. (*Peskita*, parag. 23)

14. This midrash amplifies the metaphor of the Book of Life by metaphorically commenting on the ink that God uses in order to do His writing.

When a person sins during the year, a record of his transgression is inscribed in faint ink. If that person repents during the Ten Days of Penitence, the record is erased. If not, it is written in indelible ink. (*Otzar Midrashim*, p. 494)

15. Chapter 22 of the book of Genesis contains the familiar story of the binding of Isaac. In the story (customarily read on the second day of Rosh Hashanah), Abraham is commanded to offer as a sacrifice to God his precious child Isaac. It was a supreme test of Abraham's faith in God. The following question has often been asked: If God knows all and knew that Abraham would obey, then why

would God test him in the first place? The following midrash attempts to define the true purpose of God's test.

When Isaac was about to be sacrificed, Abraham asked God, who had stayed his hand: "If You have come only to test me, surely You did know that I am ready to obey You?"

To this God responded, "I did indeed know your heart and mind but I wished to demonstrate to the peoples the reason why I am friendlier to you than to them. Moreover, when I judge your sons each year on Rosh Hashanah, I shall remember your loyalty when they sound the ram's horn, for the ram was substituted for Isaac." (*Peskita Rabbati* 41, 6)

16. In the following story, the Talmud attempts to explain the opening verse of the story of the binding of Isaac "and it was after these things, and God tested Abraham." [Genesis 22:1] The rabbis pondered the meaning of "these things," which goes undescribed in the Bible.

It is written, And it was after these things that God tested Abraham. [Genesis 22:]

After which things?

Rabbi Yochanan said in the name of Rabbi Yossi, the son of Zimra: "After the events that involved Satan. For it is written, and the boy grew up, and was weaned"... [Genesis 21:8]

"Satan said to the Holy One, blessed be He: Master of the Universe, You have allowed this old man to reach the age of one hundred. And yet, of all of the feasts he has made, he never once sacrificed before You even a single turtledove or one fledgling."

He replied: "He made these feasts in honor of the birth of his son. If I were to tell him to sacrifice that son to Me, he would surely do so."

Thereupon, and the Lord tested Abraham. [Genesis 22:1]

It is written, And God said, Please take your son, your only one, that you love, Isaac, and go to the land of Moriah, and offer him up there as a burnt offering on one of the hills that I will show you. [Genesis 22:2]

Rabbi Shimeon, the son of Abba, said: "The verse uses terms of entreaty rather than command. There is an analogy to this. A mortal king of flesh and blood was beset by many wars. He had one mighty warrior who fought these wars for him and won them all. After a time, the threat of a major war loomed.

"The king said to the warrior, I beg of you to wage this war for me so that it not be said that your earlier service was meaningless.

"So too did the Holy One, blessed be He, say to Abraham: 'I have put you through many ordeals and you have survived them all. Now I ask you to withstand this ordeal so that it not be said that the earlier ones were meaningless'...." (Talmud, *Sanhedrin* 89b)

17. Repentance is a key theme of the festival of Rosh Hashanah. Here are several midrashim related to the importance of repentance to the Jewish people:

i. Great is repentance, for it preceded even the creation of the world itself. As it is written, Before the mountains came into existence and before You brought forth the earth and the world.... You return man to dust, and you decreed "return you mortals" [Psalm 90:2–3] What was the call to repentance? A heavenly voice when cried out saying, "Repent, you children of men." (Midrash on Psalms 90:12)

ii. If a person repents he converts into pious deeds even the many sins of which he may be guilty. (*Exodus Rabbah* 31:1)

iii. Rabbi Zussya of Hanipol said: "There are five verses in the Bible which constitute the essence of Judaism. These verses begin in Hebrew with one of these letters: *'Tav, Shin, Vav, Bet, Heh,'* which comprise the Hebrew word for repentance, *teshuvah.*"

a. You shall be whole hearted with the Lord, your God. (Deuteronomy 18:13)

b. I have set God always before me. (Psalms 16:8)

c. But you shall love your neighbor as yourself. (Leviticus 19:18)

d. In all your ways acknowledge Him. (Proverbs 3:6)

e. To walk humbly with your God. (Micah 6:8)

Therefore, resolve to act accordingly, so that your repentance may be sincere. (Hasidic)

18. Signs and omens were very much a part of the rabbinic thinkers' tradition. Here are two examples of signs and omens as they relate to the festival of Rosh Hashanah.

i. Rabbi Zebid said: "If the first day of the New Year is warm, most of the year will be warm. If cold, most of the year will be cold."

ii. It has been said that omens are of significance. Therefore, a person should make a regular habit of eating, at the beginning of the year, a pumpkin, fenugreek, leek, beet, and dates [symbols of prosperity]. (Talmud, *Horayot* 12a)

19. There are many stories and legends related to the shofar, the ram's horn that is sounded on Rosh Hashanah. In the first story, we learn that each part of the original ram that was sacrificed by

Abraham in the thicket (as described in Genesis 22), was put to a purposeful use. In the second story, the secret meaning behind the blasts of the shofar is explained.

i. Rabbi Chanina ben Dosa says: No part of the ram went to waste. The ashes of the ram became the base of the inner altar. The sinews of the ram were torn, corresponding to the ten strings of the harp that David played. The skin of the ram became the girdle of Elijah's loins. As for the two horns of the ram, the voice of the left horn was heard at Mount Sinai. The horn on the right is larger than the left one and will be sounded at a future time when the dispersed are all assembled, as it is written [Isaiah 27:13]: "And it shall come to pass on that day, that a great horn shall be sounded." (*Pirke Rabbi Eliezer*, 31)

ii. Once the Baal Shem Tov commanded Rabbi Zev Kitzes to go out and discover the secret meaning behind the blasts of the shofar, because Rabbi Zev was scheduled to be his caller on Rosh Hashanah. Rabbi Zev learned the secret meanings and wrote them down on a slip of paper in order to look at them during the service. He laid the piece of paper in his bosom.

The time arrived for the blowing of the shofar, and he began to look everywhere for the piece of paper, but it had vanished, and he did not know on what meanings to concentrate. He was extremely saddened, and, weeping tears, he called the sounds of the shofar without concentrating on the secret meaning within them.

Afterward, said the Baal Shem Tov to him, "In the habitation of the king are to be found many rooms and apartments, and there are different keys for every lock. But the master key of all is the ax, with which it is possible to open all of the locks on the gates. So, too, is it with the ram's horn. The secret meanings are the keys. Every gate has another meaning, but the master key is the broken heart. When a person sincerely breaks his heart before God, such a person can enter into all of the gates of the apartments of the King of Kings, the Holy One blessed by He." (*Or Yesharim*, a folktale)

YOM KIPPUR

Yom Kippur, the Day of Atonement, generally considered the holiest day of the year, is the culmination of the Ten Days of Repentance. Also known as the Day of Judgment, its message is that human beings can change for the better and improve their character. Jewish tradition reports that on the tenth of the Hebrew month of Tishri, Moses returned from Mount Sinai with the second tablets of the Ten Commandments and announced to the people God's pardon for the sin of the golden calf.

During the periods of the Jerusalem Temple the predominant feature of the Day of Atonement was the elaborate Temple ritual, as recorded in the Bible. On Yom Kippur only the high priest entered the holy of holies to make atonement for his sins and for those of the Israelite people. Today, prayer, charity, fasting, and repentance are ways of averting God's severe decree.

Although one finds references to Yom Kippur throughout the Talmud, the tractate entitled *Yoma* is devoted by and large to this holy day. The selections below are talmudic and midrashic sources that relate to Yom Kippur.

1. The following midrashim explain the origins of the Day of Atonement.

i. From the inception of the creation of the world, the Holy One, blessed be He, foresaw the actions of both the righteous and wicked. "And the earth was desolate" alludes to the deeds of the wicked people. "And God said: Let there be light" refers to the righteous ones. "And God made a division between the light and darkness" refers to the division between the deeds of the righteous and the deeds of the wicked. "And God called the light day" foreshadows the deeds of the righteous. "And the darkness God called night" refers to the deeds of the wicked. "And there was evening" refers to the deeds of the wicked. "And there was morning" refers to the deeds of the righteous. And the phrase "one day" refers to the fact that the Holy One gave the people one day. Which day was that? It is the Day of Atonement. (*Genesis Rabbah* 3:10)

ii. When the Israelites received the Ten Commandments on the festival of Shavuot, Moses ascended Mount Sinai and stayed there for forty days in order to receive the tablets of the Law. On the seventeenth of the month of Tammuz he came down from the mountain, and seeing the people worshipping the golden calf, he broke the tablets. Then, for forty days, Moses pitched his tent beyond the camp, and the people grieved. On the first day of the month of Elul, Moses again ascended the mountain to receive the second tablets. During this time the Israelites fasted from the rising of the sun of its setting. This day was the tenth of Tishri. When Moses returned in the morning, the Israelites went to meet him. Moses saw them weeping, and he too cried because he was aware that they were in a state of penitence. God then said, "Your repentance is acceptable to me, and this day will remain the Day of Atonement throughout all generations." (*Eliyahu Zuta,* 4)

iii. "And God call the light day" [Genesis 1:5] is symbolic of Jacob. "And the darkness God called night" symbolizes Esau. "And there was evening" symbolizes Esau. "And there was morning" symbolizes Jacob. "One day" teaches that the Holy One, blessed be He, gave him one special day. Which day is that? It is the Day of Atonement. (*Genesis Rabbah* 2, 3)

iv. Of the three hundred and sixty five days of the year, the Holy One already had designated one of them as His very own. Which day was that? Rabbi Levi and Rabbi Isaac had different opinions. Rabbi Levi said that it was the Day of Atonement, basing his opinion on the verse "Is such the fast that I have chosen, the day for a person to afflict his soul?" [Isaiah 58:5] Rabbi Isaac, however, said that it was the day of the Sabbath. (*Pesikta Rabbati* 23, 1)

2. In the following midrash the observance of the Day of Atonement saves a Jew from certain danger.

Rabbi Pinchas tells the story of a righteous man in Rome who used to always honor the holy days and the Sabbath. On the eve of the Sabbath—some say it was the evening of the Great Fast [i.e., the Day of Atonement]—the pious man went to the market to buy something. The only thing that he found to buy was one single fish.

A servant of the governor was also there at the market, and he too wanted the fish. And so, each bid for it against the other. Finally, the Jew won the bid and bought the fish at one dinar per pound.

As the time drew near for the meal, the governor remarked to his servant, "There is no fish."

Replied the servant, "Only one fish was available for purchase at the market, and a Jew bought it at one dinar per pound."

"Do you know the Jew?" asked the governor. The servant replied, "Yes."

The governor then told his servant to bring the Jew to him, thinking that he likely owned a treasure that must belong to the king.

The servant summoned the Jew, and brought him forth to the governor.

The governor asked, "Who are you?" The man replied, "I am a Jew."

The governor then asked, "What is your profession?" The Jew responded, "I am a tailor."

The governor then asked, "But is there a tailor that can really afford to eat food that costs one dinar per pound?"

The Jew responded, "If I am given permission, I would like to say something to you in my defense." The governor replied, "Speak!"

The Jew said, "We Jewish people, have one day which is dearer to us than all of the other days of the year. This special day atones for all of the transgressions which we have committed during the year, allowing us to be forgiven. It is thus that we honor it more than any other single day of the year."

The governor replied, "Since you have brought a reason for what you have done, I must let you go free."

How did the Holy One, blessed be He, repay the tailor? He caused him to find in the fish a jewel of purest ray, a pearl. And for the money he received for it, he lived well for the rest of his life. (*Pesikta Rabbati* 23, 6)

3. Making atonement for one's sins is one of the true purposes of the Day of Atonement. The following midrashim illustrate various rabbinic interpretations of the act of making atonement.

i. There was once a province that owed arrears to the king, and the king came to collect them. Approaching the province and within ten miles of it, nobility of the province came out and praised him. The king then freed them of one-third of their tax burden.

When he was within five miles, the middle class came out and also offered praise to the king. He then freed them of another third of their tax burden.

When he finally entered the province all of the people, men, women, and children came out to praise him. The king then freed them of the entire sum saying, "Let bygones be bygones. From now on we shall begin for you a new account."

In a similar manner, on the eve of the New Year, the leaders of the generation fast, and the Holy One, blessed be He, forgives them of one-third of their sins. From New Year to the Day of Atonement, private individuals fast, and the Holy One, blessed be He, absolves them of a third of their sins. On Yom Kippur, everybody fasts, men, women, and children, and the Holy One, blessed be He, says to Israel, "Let bygones be bygones. From now on we shall begin a new account." (*Leviticus Rabbah* 30:7)

ii. If a nut falls into some dirt, a person can pick it up, wipe it off, and rinse and wash it in order to restore it to its prior condition so that it can be eaten. Similarly, no matter how much the children of Israel are defiled with transgression all the rest of the year, when the Day of Atonement comes, it makes atonement for them, as it is written, "for on this day shall atonement be made for you, to cleanse you." [Leviticus 16:30] (*Song of Songs Rabbah* 6, 11)

iii. On Yom Kippur Satan comes to accuse the Israelites and he specifies the sins of Israel. Satan says, "Master of the Universe, there are adulterers among the nations of the earth. So too, they are among Israel."

What does God do? He suspends the beam of the scales and looks to see what the balance looks like between the sins and the righteous deeds. And as they are weighed, the two pans of the scale show an exact balance between the sins and the good deeds.

Satan then proceeds to acquire more sins to put in the pan of transgressions in order to bring it down. What does the Holy One, blessed be He, then do? While Satan is seeking out sins, the Holy One, blessed be He, takes the sins out of the pan and hides them under His royal purple. When Satan returns he finds no sin at all on the scale, as it is said, "The iniquity of Israel shall be sought, and there shall be none." (Jeremiah 50:20) (*Pesikta Rabbata* 45, 2)

iv. The number value of the Hebrew letters in *ha-Satan* [the Satan] the Adversary, is three hundred and sixty four, which is one less than the total number of days in the year. Thus the Adversary is given the authority to make accusations against the Israelites on all of the days of the year, with the exception of the Day of Atonement. On this day, the Holy One, blessed be He, says to Satan, "You have no authority to touch them. However, go and see how they occupy themselves."

The Adversary obeys and goes to the Israelites. He finds them all fasting and praying, dressed in white clothing like ministering angels. Confused and ashamed, he goes back.

The Holy One, blessed be He, then asks him, "What have you discovered about My children?" Satan responds, "They are like ministering angels, and I am not able to touch them."

Then the Holy One, blessed be He, chains the Adversary and declares to the Israelites, "I have forgiven you." (Midrash on Psalms 27, 4)

v. Rabbi Bibi, the son of Abaye, said: "How should a person make confession on Yom Kippur? He should say, 'I confess all the evil that I had done before you. I stood in the way of evil, and I shall do no more evil again. May it be Your will, O God, that You should grant pardon for all of my sins.' This is indicated by what is written, Let the wicked forsake his way and the person of iniquity his thoughts.' " [Isaiah 55:7]

Rabbi Isaac and Rabbi Jose ben Chanina each presented an analogy. Rabbi Isaac said, "It is like a man fitting together two boards, and rejoining them one to another." Rabbi Jose ben Chanina said, "It is like a man fitting two bed legs together and joining them." (*Leviticus Rabbah* 3, 3)

4. The following midrash expresses the greatness of the power of making peace and forgiving one another. It concludes by reiterating a change in God's language. Sarah had reported that her husband Abraham was old, but God, in quoting Sarah, revises the statement to include Sarah's old age as well. In this way, God Himself attempts to preserve the peace by not having Abraham embarrassed by Sarah's statement.

May the name of God be praised and His title honored. For in God's care of Israel, He ordained the Ten Days of Repentance for them, so that if even a single person of the congregation of Israel repents, that repentance is accepted as though it were the repentance of the entire congregation.

Therefore all of the congregation of Israel should hold fast to repentance. Let each of them make peace with the other and forgive one another on the Day of Atonement, in order that the Holy One, blessed be He, accept their repentance and prayer with love and in reconciliation.

The power of peace is so great among people that it is for its sake that even the Holy One, blessed be He, revises the words a person has spoken. For instance, in the passage, "and Sarah laughed within herself, saying ... 'Shall I have pleasure, my lord also being old?'" [Genesis 18:12], but to Abraham God said: "Why did Sarah laugh, saying, 'Shall I in truth bear a child, old as I am?'" But God revised her words, having her say "old as I am," in order that no bad feelings should arise between Abraham and Sarah because of her calling him old. (*Peskita Rabbati* 50:6)

5. The following three stories present a methodology for atoning for one's sins—offering deeds of kindness. The Talmud (*Berachot* 6b) has said that "the merit of a fast day lies in the deeds of righteousness that are dispensed."

i. One time Rabbi Yochanan ben Zakkai was coming from Jerusalem, and Rabbi Joshua followed him. In seeing the Temple in ruins Rabbi Joshua cried, "Woe to us, that this place where Israel made atonement for its sins has been laid to waste."

"My son," Rabbi Yochanan said to him, "do not despair. We have another kind of atonement that is just as effective as this. And what might it be? Deeds of kindness, as it is written, 'for I desire mercy and not sacrifice.' " [Hosea 6:6]

We also find that concerning Daniel, an exceedingly beloved man, that he too was engaged in deeds of kindness.

What were the acts of kindness in which he was occupied? Can you say that he offered burnt offerings and sacrifices in Babylon? What were the deeds of kindness in which he was involved? He used to outfit the bride and make her rejoice. He was accustomed to accompanying the dead and giving a *perutah* to poor people. He also was accustomed to pray three times daily, and his prayer was always received favorably. (*Avot de Rabbi Natan*, 4)

ii. When the Jerusalem Temple stood, a person used to bring his shekel in order to make atonement. Now that the Temple no longer exists, if they give for charity, all well and good. If not, the heathens will come and take from them forcibly. Even so, it will be reckoned to them as if they had given charity. (Talmud, *Baba Batra* 9a)

iii. Mar Ukba had a poor person in his community to whom he regularly sent four hundred *zuzim* on the eve of every Yom Kippur. Once, he sent them through his son, who came back and said to him "He doesn't need your help."

"What is it that you have seen?" his father asked.

"I saw that they were setting old wine before him."

"Is he so delicate?" asked the father. And he sent back his son with twice the usual amount. (Talmud, *Ketubot* 67b)

FOR FURTHER READING

Agnon, S. Y. *Days of Awe.* New York: Schocken Books, 1948.

Bloch, Abraham P. *The Biblical and Historical Background of Jewish Holy Days.* New York: Ktav Publishers, 1978.

Chill, Abraham. The *Minhagim.* New York: Sepher Hermon Press, 1979.

Eisemann, Moshe. *The Theme of the High Holy Days Machzor.* New York: Art Scroll, 1993.

Frankel, Ellen. *The Classic Tales.* Northvale, N. J.: Jason Aronson, 1989.

Ganzfield, Solomon. *Code of Jewish Law.* New York: Hebrew Publishing Company, 1961.

Gaster, Theodor H. *Festivals of the Jewish Year.* New York: William Morrow and Company, 1952.

Jacobs, Louis. *A Guide to Yom Kippur.* London: Jewish Chronicles Publications, 1951.

Kitov, Eliyahu. *The Book of Our Heritage.* Translated by Nathan Bulman. Jerusalem and New York: Feldheim Publishers, 1970.

Rosenfeld, Abraham. *The Authorised Selichot for the Whole Year.* London: Labworth and Company, 1956.

Schauss, Hayyim. *Guide to the Jewish Holy Days.* New York: Schocken Books, 1938.

Vainstein, Yaacov. *The Cycle of the Jewish Year: A Study of the Festivals and Selections from the Liturgy.* Jerusalem: World Zionist Organization, 1964.

Waskow, Arthur. *Seasons of Our Joy.* New York: Summit Books, 1982.

INDEX

Book of Life, 48, 66, 85, 113, 182, 185
Book of Records, 56
Buber, Martin, 37

Chanina, R., 176, 183
Chanina b. Dosa, R., 189
Channah, 66, 177–78
Chayei Adam, 64
Chayim, R. of Zans, 75–76, 179–80
Chilkiah, R., 181
Code of Jewish Law, 3, 4, 9, 61, 103
Commandments, second tablets of, 174, 191
Community responsibility, 75–76
Confession, 27–28
  Jewish, 27
  rabbinic quotations relating to, 27–28
Covenant, night of remembering, 174
Crusade, period of the first, 162

Daniel, 197
David, 183–84
Day of Atonement, 44, 85, 89, 144, 190–97 See also Yom Kippur
  spirit of, 161
Day of Judgment, 40, 44, 190
  preparations for, 175

Day of Remembrance, 40
Days of Awe, xi, 40, 112–13
  in Jewish legend, 173–90
Days of Penitence, 85–87, 185
Days of Repentance, 176, 190, 196

Egypt, bondage in, 66, 178
Eleh Ezkera Service, 162–63
Elhanan, 76–79
Eliezer, R., 43, 45, 121–22, 177–79, 184
Eliezer b. Hyrcanus, R., 30
Elijah, 171–72
Elul, month of, 2, 9, 17, 36, 174, 191
  charity during, 2
  prayer during, 2–3
  as preparation for Rosh Hashanah, 1
  repentence during, 1–6
  shofar sounded during, 9
Ephraim, 129
Erev Rosh Hashanah, 4–6
  customs associated with, 5–6
Esau, 191
Ethics of the Fathers, 26
Evil inclination, 25–26
Ezekiel, 29
Ezra the Scribe, 42, 46

Fasting, 6, 99, 175–76, 194
Festival of Booths, 40 See also Sukkot

About the Author

Rabbi Ronald H. Isaacs is the spiritual leader of Temple Sholom in Bridgewater, New Jersey. He received his doctorate in instructional technology from Columbia University's Teacher's College. He is the author of numerous books, including *Loving Companions: Our Jewish Wedding Album*, co-authored with Leora Isaacs. Rabbi Isaacs currently serves on the editorial board of *Shofar* magazine and is a member of the Publications Committee of the Rabbinical Assembly. He resides in New Jersey with his wife, Leora, and their children, Keren and Zachary.